HOW TO BE A FIT MUM

15 WAYS TO HAVE-IT-ALL

STEFANIA IANCU

Published by Stefania Iancu

ISBN- 978-1-78926-582-8

Printed in the United Kingdom
Cover design by Olivier Kili
First Edition

CONTENTS

Acknowledgement

This book would not have been possible without the full support of my partner, Oli, and my therapist, Andreea. My son, this book healed me and made me a better mom. I did it for you, baby, Mummy loves you.

Introduction

Who picks up a book titled How To Be a Fit Mum? My guess is you are certainly a mother who wants more from her current life. Despite the fitness allure, this book will help you become fit in every single area of your life. One of my all-time favourite quote is this: "An unfit mother is a selfish mother."
You may get shocked by this statement. Well, it means this book might not be for you.

You can put it down or return it for a happy refund. If on the other end, you are curious and want to discovery what your body and mind are truly capable on achieving then read on.

What to expect from this book: a roadmap to your complete transformation starting right this moment. You will learn from my life experiences and the ones from several mothers who are now truly empowered. Once you finish this book, your CHANGE will begin! Subconsciously, your mind and body will get you ready to start your healing.
There is a reason why I chose to share my complete journey with you, instead of a nutrition and training plan. Right now you go online and type "weight loss", you get over 70 million results. Access to information is fast and free. Anything you need to

know is out there, a click away. And yet your wheels are not moving in the right direction. You are more depressed and overweight than ever. You doubt your ability to achieve because there has been too much failure.

You are lacking motivation. You seem to never finish what you start. And with every failed attempt you get even more frustrated. I know exactly how you feel, I have been there, I have been you. That feeling you get several times per day, that maybe that's how you were meant to be and you want to give up on yourself. That's the most hopeless, painful feeling one can have... to give up on yourself! I want to help you defeat all your fears and let go of the pain so you never, ever, ever again feel this horrible, breathtaking feeling of giving up on yourself.

The book is based on my personal life and experiences. It is a sad story with an ongoing healing process, because becoming better is a daily norm and as long as I breathe I learn. It all started with embarking on a weight loss journey to soon discover that there were deeper wounds which prevented me from reaching happiness and satisfaction in life.

Chapter 1

Assume responsibility

Despite what you've been told for decades, losing weight is not about food or exercise. That actually follows after you have made the initial decision to take care of yourself and become better. You live an unhealthy life because of a learnt behaviour or a traumatic event that shaped your current life. Once I took responsibility for my choices and stopped putting the blame on everyone and everything else I was able to move forward. Letting go of the emotional burden of the past allowed me to live a brilliant present.

Most obese children come from families with obese parents. Most sedentary children come from families where nobody moves a finger for their health. It is a behavioural pattern which unfortunately is passed on from generation to generation. And as an adult you wonder how you got there and why life is so unfair that you are overweight or obese. The question shouldn't be how you got there, but what are you willing to do to fix it? I have blamed my parents for my weight issues my whole life. With every occasion I got I would tell them how they had ruined my life and how their laziness and lack of nutritional knowledge made me obese. As a child I would always get double portions of food: two bananas, two packs of biscuits, two ice creams, you name it. It was always double. And trust me, I would finish it all without breathing. The real problem was that my portions were increasing at an amazing pace. By the time I was sixteen years old, I was eating more than my twenty-six year old brother.

As an adult I was still pointing at my parents for being obese. It felt only fair on my side to keep emphasising why I looked that way. Until the day when I had my epiphany moment. That's when I realised that my life was actually driven by negative emotions. Hate, frustration, disappointment, you name it. I had literally given up on myself and my ability to make my life better. Instead of having a 'what would make me happy' attitude, I was fully absorbed in a 'it is your fault for being this way' attitude. Even now I still believe it was their fault. Every second of pain that I went through in my life, it was their fault. However, as an adult I was faced with two options: to keep blaming them for my obesity and be forever unhappy, or to truly grow up and take control of my life. I had to sit down and have a long chat with my inner child. You know how kids scream, throw themselves on the floor and express their frustration very strongly and loudly?

That's exactly the kind of emotional turmoil I was still experiencing. Although as a grown up I knew what I was supposed to do to live a better life, my inner child was really wounded and was holding me back from making smarter choices.

A person who has experienced weight issues her whole life has gathered a lot of pain. Despite all the information available on how to live a better life, you seem to be unable to truly stay focused on your goal. That's because being obese is the outcome of an inner pain, not the other way around, and in the hope that the pain will miraculously disappear you keep on binge eating. Take it from somebody who has tried to eat and drown her pain in alcohol, you will never get that emotional numbness you are so desperately hoping for. Instead of seeking some kind of addiction that could finally release you of your emotional burden, start looking into your pain. It can be hidden or it can be obvious. Regardless, you are the only one who can pick up the pieces and control your emotions.

As I mentioned above, your overeating could be caused by unhealthy eating habits developed since childhood or by traumatic events. In my family, my dad was the abuser. I was lucky enough to have an amazing mom, the greatest mom in the world, who invested enough in me to give me the opportunity to be better and act accordingly in life. Because I had only one parent as an abuser, I could be saved! My abuse was emotional, psychological and physical. As I write these lines I feel physical discomfort (my stomach is twisting and my throat closes) and huge emotional distress. But I have to do it. Being able to talk freely about my past is part of my healing journey. I have friends and family who don't know anything about my abuse and will find out after reading this book and probably feel sorry for me. I don't want or need that because I am not that little scared girl anymore. I have become a strong woman capable of protecting herself and her family.

I do want you to understand the pain I grew up with. I was scared something would trigger his anger at all times. From a window left open at night to watching TV too loud, if he was in a mood to scream and fight nothing could stop him. I was living under constant terror. And food was my salvation. I was overeating in the hope that my pain would disappear, that somehow all his abuses would stop and I could live a carefree life. I was three or four years old and I was craving sweets (perfectly normal for that age). And since my parents were asleep, I thought I should help myself and take money from the upper shelf where the money was held. There were two problems: one, I didn't know the value of money, and secondly, some older girls from my neighbourhood advised me to take way more money than I needed (money which they took from me of course).

One day my parents were doing their finances and found there was money missing. As you can imagine all the children were interrogated several times, because no one would admit. Nobody expected the youngest one to be guilty. In the end I confessed and I got one of the worst beatings of my life. I remember my abuser throwing me on the bed at some point, bringing out a knife and asking me to hold my hands up. And he put the bloody blade on my wrists and swore to me that if a similar episode happens ever again he will cut off my hands. Even now if I find one penny in my parents' house I will not touch it. I had nightmares with that knife for years and the trauma has never left me. It was not my fault. I was three years old – all I wanted was ice cream and chocolate. I have never meant to upset and disappoint anybody, not to mention steal. My intentions were pure and genuine, but my actions were misinterpreted by an adult who did not take a minute to understand my age, my intellect and my emotional status. And because of that he abused his position and inflicted physical and emotional pain on a three year old! I remember my mom crying and telling him to leave me alone because 'she is only a child'.

The longer the trauma, the less likely your demons will leave you. I know they rest inside me and wait for me to become weak and vulnerable and take control over me. I have worked really hard to control myself and to understand every emotion, thought and action I experience or undertake. Despite the constant fear that in moments of vulnerability I may overeat again, I know now I am much stronger than before. By learning your true value you don't have to fear hardship anymore. The new you will be able to develop healthy coping mechanisms and take constructive steps to get over the unforeseen circumstances. It is very unlikely for you to resort to food anymore, because now you are aware of how strong you really are.

Life is not fair by all means. Obstacles, abuses, unforeseen events, accidents, God's acts, you never know what your present or future will bring. The stronger you are the better coping mechanisms you develop. When the hard times come again you will be ready. Letting go of your past and seeing your true value will inevitably make you stronger. The reason why I share my past with you is not because I haven't healed. Quite the opposite. As you go through this book you will discover a confident woman who made has peace with her past. The scars rarely disappear but the memories and the hate have faded. And by closing this chapter of my life I was able to find happiness and love. Without healing I would have never allowed myself to love my partner.

Assuming ownership over your life is liberating. It's literally like being reborn. The moment I stopped looking back and finding others guilty for my pain I evolved into an amazing person. When you hold on to your pain you can't move forward. I left home when I was nineteen. I came to the UK to study law. I was 1,500 miles away from my abuser and yet I was still living a sad life. I was still overeating and drinking too much. After a life of abuses, regardless how far away my body was geographically, the pain had become me. I was the pain! I couldn't escape it. I grew up with an abusive father and I became obese in my attempt to numb my pain through food. As an adult I had failed to take responsibility and I was living in the past.

Your pain can have different shapes and be caused by a multitude of factors. What all victims have in common is the inability to escape or let go of the past. First step to recovery is acceptance. Accept whatever happened to you and stop being a victim. Once you quit moaning and take positive steps to improve the quality of your life, you will be able to gain control over it. Secondly, be honest with yourself. How has any addiction helped you defeat your pain so far? The opposite. By hurting your body even more, you added more frustration and disappointment to your current pain. Thirdly, don't shift the blame from the abuser to you. You haven't made the best choices in the past, let's say. And now you are at a point where you want to give up on yourself because you are the adult. Don't be too harsh on yourself. You have tried your best to cope with the situation and every decision you have made seemed appropriate at that time. The fourth step is to assume full responsibility for the way you currently live your life.

Life is not about short cuts. It is not possible to skip steps in your transformation journey. Remember this: everything that comes easy will be underappreciated. So when you go to bed crying and begging for life to have it easy on you, remember that life only tests the strong ones. It never gives you more than you can handle. As ironic as it sounds, when you emerge from your pain you will be unstoppable. A superwoman will be reborn and this time you will dictate your own terms.

Summary

The first step to weight loss is finding your inner pain. Work out your emotions and develop healthy coping mechanisms. Forgive yourself for your failure to do better and start making smarter choices today. The easiest thing to do is blame your mess on somebody else. Do you truly think that people who seem to have it all in life don't face difficulties? Of course they do.

Life will test your strengths and weaknesses. Life will give you a chance to choose – it is you who makes the final call. If so far you have been fully immersed in the victims' attitude, it is time to take responsibility for your life and make grown-up decisions. You are the only one who can improve the quality of your life. The emotional mess you are in right now can only be overcome by you.

Chapter 2

Self-doubt

My whole life I wanted to believe in myself. Fat or skinny, living a great life or one full of struggles, all I wanted was to find some value in myself. I wanted to believe that I was capable of greatness and that I could achieve everything on my list. Unfortunately, it took me over a decade to discover the real me. Who I am, what I stand for, what I believe in, what my strengths and weaknesses are. And in this process I have learnt many things about myself, and the knowledge I gathered in my hardest times has proved to be my most powerful tool in the fight against self-doubt and insecurity.

As a baby you don't hate yourself. You cry when you are sick, hungry, tired, need a nappy change, feel scared and so forth. You cry to raise awareness of your discomfort so your mummy can care for you. It's called survival. I believe there is more to it. Getting a nappy change is not a matter of survival, but comfort. And you can feel you mum's love, care and happiness when she can make you feel better. And growing up in that kind of environment will do something wonderful for you in the future: it will build the foundation for you to love yourself. Knowing love, feeling truly loved, is empowering. I have only discovered unconditional love when I met the father of my son. I know my mum loves me enormously, but she was so busy as I grew up that she forgot to show it or take the time to make me feel it again, like when I was little.

Well, my partner understands my need to feel loved. I don't want a platonic love, you know it is there, I want an active love. I want it to flow through my veins, I want love to be too much. As you grow up you become subject to harsh criticism – most of the time parents don't take the time to understand why kids do certain things and will jump straight in to crush the kids' feelings. That's good parenting when the child is too scared to talk back (sarcasm). And that is the beginning of you experiencing self-doubt and insecurity.

Let's talk about school, church, extended family members, everybody has an opinion about you and how you should live your life. And when you are young you let all that in. And as time passes the pile of advice and criticism becomes too heavy and you learn hate. Self-hate. In school you have to thrive to be the best at everything you study. In sports you must outperform all your peers. Religion asks you to live a sin free life or you go to hell or will be punished somehow by a divinity. Aunties and uncles are the worst. They can speak forever. Their nonsense never stops and it is disrespectful to stand up and tell them how much you really don't care.

I need to pause here and tell you a story. I was ten years old and I don't know these days but back in the 1990s religion was a proper subject in school. And our teacher decided to take us for our first communion. The walk there was fun and all, although I wasn't sure what was happening. Oh, I have to mention I was raised in an Orthodox family. When you go to church to confess your naughty lifestyle you kneel and put your head under the priest's church clothing, whatever that thing is called. I am not much of a religious person anyway. So you can see already how you are inferior and human compared to the highly gifted priest who sits or stands and weighs in your outrageous behaviour. And the priest told me that if I spit it is a sin. If I think bad about people it is a sin. If I get angry with my parents it is a sin... there were too many sins for me to remember them all. I left my communion terrified. I went home and told Mum there is no hope for me because I cannot control my thoughts and God will punish me heavily. Obviously Mum's reaction was priceless and she explained to me that religion is more complicated than that, so go and play and forget it.

Some say it is a gift, others say it is a curse. I always speak my mind and always share the truth. If I hadn't had that conversation with Mum and had her reassurance that I am amazing and that priest was talking nonsense, just think what that event could have caused. The emotional burden it put on me, as a child, for being unable to control my thoughts or anger was huge. As you can imagine it was my first and last communion. I was never able to get over the manipulation and lack of consideration of that priest.

And in life episodes like this are recurrent. You will eventually become a grown up full of self-doubt and insecurity. Because you can't match other people's standards, you fail to see your true value. There was so much imposing on you, so much influence, that you were not allowed to be yourself anymore. I am a highly active woman. I have been like this since birth, it is in my DNA. However, my environment couldn't keep up with me. The solution? I would get beaten until I would stay still. It sounds crazy, doesn't it? Well, back in those days beating was the best educating tool, according to... pretty much everybody who lived in those times. So I would get beaten not because I was misbehaving or did something to deserve it, but as a preventive measure of what I could have potentially caused with my running around. I am a fighter and I never stop from claiming what I believe is right. I didn't allow all this beating to change who I was, but it did prevent me from living to my full potential. They inhibited my restless side and tried to make me live by their rules, even if they had to use force.

After each beating I would say to myself, 'why can't you just be like them? Why can't you meet their standards? Why can't you comply with authority?'

And all these thoughts and all their attempts to prevent me from being myself lead to one thing: my deep belief that I am not good enough and I am a disappointment. When you doubt yourself that is not you. That is the outcome of all the influences in your life. There is somebody else out there doubting himself and passing that on to you. When you grow up in a hostile environment, love and acceptance seem to be truly far away from you. I know for sure that you were born to be amazing. You were born to be who you want to be. Your environment, however, had different plans for you and you had to fit in. That meant inhibiting some of your qualities, disabling some of your strengths and living a life which doesn't make you happy. And the failure to achieve what you were born to achieve comes at a price. Unfortunately, you are paying the price for their ignorance.

Self-doubt starts at an early age. It's small decisions you have to make as a child or teenager, and then as you age things are getting serious. You want a good job, a great family, a big house, a dog, a tree, at least one holiday per year, a happy marriage, perfect kids and the standards keep going up. But as you progress in life things don't always work out as planned. And that's when all your insecurities and self-doubts surface.

When major decisions are to be taken and great things are to be accomplished, that's when you realise that you are unable to deal with failure. And the only reason why failure is the first thought on your mind is because of self-doubt. Losing weight has been my main battle since I was nine years old. That's correct, I started my first diet at nine years old. Mum got me an appointment with a very thin and old female doctor. She checked my weight and measurements thoroughly and gave her diagnosis: I was overweight. Solution? Put a nine year old on a strict weight loss diet. And I do emphasise here, DIET. She didn't bother to explain to Mum how to feed me healthier foods for example. Or steps to take to improve the eating habits in the house. Oh no, I was given a very low calorie diet, which, looking back, was completely unsustainable long-term.

Morale? Read and learn more about nutrition and how to before doing weight loss experiments. Or have somebody teach you. I followed that diet for about three months. I did lose some weight of course, but before I knew it I was hiding in my room to eat junk so nobody could see me. In my head, if my parents were to find out I was eating I would disappoint them so badly that I wouldn't be able to live with it. Of course they knew I was hiding to eat since I was gaining weight again. Trying and failing at such an early age, plus the outside pressure, made me doubt myself.

I felt like a letdown. I felt weak. I felt like a quitter. I felt I was not worthy of love or respect. That's what a failed weight loss diet can do to a child. It was so painful to answer questions like 'weren't you on a diet'? 'have you gained the weight back'? 'why are you eating chocolate'? 'can't you see you are fluffy, why are you eating again'? Believe it or not those were the kind of things I would get asked at nine years old. Hurray! That's what I call a childhood full of love and support. This failure weighted heavy in my decision that I am not worthy of much. That my body is completely 'wrong' and I will never reach the physical standards imposed by my environment. Self-doubt is generated by your deep belief that no matter what you do, you cannot reach your own or somebody else's standards. You are not good enough to take on a challenge and succeed.

With this kind of mindset it comes as no surprise that I kept on failing diet after diet. And with every new failure I would think less of myself. You have to open your eyes and see your life for what it really is. You must acknowledge your true value and unleash your potential. The only other option you have is to keep on living a life full of failure and underappreciation. The pain of an overweight woman is highly underestimated by society. A skinny person is like 'you could eat less'. Men would say 'why don't you take care of yourself'. Your friends keep on feeding you junk food to show you love. Aunties and uncles emphasise how 'nobody will marry you'. Everybody has some piece of advice, but nobody really knows what it's like to be obese in this time and age, when free speech and social media allow endless psychological abuses.

As I mentioned in the previous chapter, a woman is not obese by choice. Whatever her burden is, she is eating in the hope to reduce the pain. An obese woman is suffering every time she looks at herself in the mirror. An obese woman hates looking at her own pictures. An obese woman finishes her shopping in tears – because nothing fits her. An obese woman is the subject of jokes. An obese woman doesn't believe in herself anymore.

When you hate your body you hate yourself. You hate that you can't make better choices. You hate that you consider yourself unworthy. And people fail to see this deep pain because you don't show it. You pretend you want to be overweight, you give reasons as to why you are this way, you hide your tears from others. You fear that exposing yourself would make you vulnerable. If you are lucky enough to come from obese parents, that's it. You will use the genetics excuse for the rest of your life. I used it too. And the more I used it the more I believed it was true. And once you have this conviction it is extremely hard to escape it. People would say, 'you are so young and you have a beautiful face, why don't you do something about your body?' Because I was born to be fat. Blame it on my parents, it is their fault for having bad genetics. And then you go even further. You will mention your aunties, uncles, grandparents, cousins, every single obese person in your close or extended family. What you are missing in this conviction is their eating habits. I doubt they all eat healthily and exercise regularly. I doubt they treat their bodies right.

In my family 95% of them are overweight or obese. It took me many years to observe their eating habits and lack of exercise. I had to grow up and understand the basics of nutrition to be able to see them for who they are. Many times they would eat leftovers from dinner or have chocolate cake for breakfast. The meals are random and never scheduled. The portion of food is at least double than normal. And they all love traditional food, which of course contains lots of deep fried food and bad fats. Oh, and sweets. The more the better. I am surprised they are not even heavier with this kind of nutrition. As I grew up I adhered to the same eating habits. I would eat randomly, sometimes even at night, and I would eat immense portions and all the deep fried food you can think of. I also developed a chocolate addiction. I was able to eat boxes of chocolate through the day. I was eating so much chocolate that on my birthday one year a friend got me a proper big box with 100 chocolates in it. It is obvious it was not genetics but my eating habits which made me obese. Since I managed to change my lifestyle and drop all the extra weight my stance on genetics has changed completely.

It sucks growing up in a family with weight issues. Not only will you most likely end up overweight, but you believe that you cannot do any better because it is written in you DNA. Genetics matter to a certain extent. You can control your genetics by making healthier choices. You can break the chain of obesity by understanding that your weight issues are rooted in the eating habits learnt from your family and that you do have the ability to make better choices.

Every time you fail to lose weight or gain it back after a diet your self-doubt increases. Every new diet or exercise you have tried so far has given you short-term results. Once you returned to your old habits you gained all the weight back. I know how badly you wish to eat anything you want and have the ideal looks at the same time. And that's how you start hating skinny people who don't have to worry about their nutrition at all. What you miss in this equation is your health. Just because somebody is a small size, it doesn't mean that all that junk and processed food she eats provides her with a strong body. I know plenty of small framed women who eat whatever and they are always tired, bloated, their skin is greasy and full of spots, they have no stamina and they are depressed. As you gather more knowledge about your body and nutrition, you will come to realise that looks are actually secondary to your health.

It is easier to say I want to lose weight to be a size eight than accept that you are scared your health might be endangered, that your kids don't see you as a role model, that you have no confidence left, that you cannot feel comfortable in your own skin. It doesn't matter what you say to the outside world as long as you know the truth. But you are scared to acknowledge your truth. You know it will hurt so you are trying to stay away from the real reason why you must change. If you want to overcome self-doubt you must overcome your pain. Find it, accept it and get closure. Being honest with yourself is one of the secrets of successful weight loss.

I thought all I wanted was to be slim. I truly believed my pain was generated by my obesity. I was so wrong. My obesity was generated by my pain. Once I understood that and I took steps to heal, my food addiction decreased and thus I was shedding the weight. Sorting out your emotions will help you get control over your binge eating. When I was living with my abuser I was stressed all the time. I was always looking around to make sure everything is in order and nothing would trigger his anger. Of course he would always find something to scream about, to threaten, to use force. Deep down I knew it wasn't my fault, and no matter how hard I would try to control everything he would still abuse me. So I turned to food. I was overeating to block out my emotions, my fear, my pain, my inability to make it stop. I was comforting myself with food since the parent who was supposed to love and protect me was terrorising me. Food became my best friend. I was eating so I wouldn't say something back and make it worse. I was eating because I was too scared to stand up for myself. I was eating to keep my sanity and not choke on my pain.

And that's how I fell victim to this never ending cycle. Comfort eating would lead to more weight gain and more weight would lead to depression. And before you know it you are an adult who is obese, depressed, unhappy, missing out on the greatest opportunities that life has to offer.

Only after I had the courage to stand up for myself and confront my abuser, I truly defeated binge eating. That was the best day of my life. I felt I could breathe again. I felt free, as if all the mental chains had been removed. It's the day I took full control over my life. I doubted myself for twenty-two years, when actually I was never the problem. The ability to be great was always inside me. My abuser had buried it to ensure control over the little weak girl.

Whatever your story is, trust me, your day will come. As long as you don't give up and have a burning desire to be better, to feel better and to look better, you will succeed. It doesn't matter how many times you have tried, never give up. Weight loss is not about diets and exercise. Weight loss is about controlling your emotions and your mental state. Your capacity to overcome the pain, get closure and move on towards a greater you.

Summary

Self-doubt starts at a very young age. Your inability to meet the requirements of your environment will have a great impact on you. School, church, family, they all play a role in your formation. Unfortunately, you become the sum of all these influences and lose touch with the real you. And every decision you make against yourself or what you believe in will increase your self-doubt.

Whatever failure you experienced in the past, don't let it shadow your present. Listen, stuff happens all the time. There is no person in this world who has a perfect, smooth existence. It is your choice if you want to dig deeper and find your pain, or keep failing and feeling like a complete disappointment. You are capable of achieving the wildest dreams you might have. You have the ability to make yourself happy. You have the ability to get your body in perfect shape.

You are the only one in full control of your life!

Chapter 3

How I lost 90 pounds

After years of punishing myself and always trying stupid short cuts to lose the extra weight, I found my path. It was my own body which sent me the final warnings that something must be done. It was the beginning of June 2013 and my health was falling apart.

I was 220 pounds at that point. My height is five feet. Yes, I did look like a ball. It was a lot of extra weight to walk around with. At this point in my life I had given up on myself completely. I felt I had lost control over my weight and there was nothing I could have done. I accepted my fat life and the pain that came with it. I was so fat that nobody would tell me to lose weight anymore. They were finally ashamed to advise me. I have a really good friend, Slavic, and he has always been honest with me. I know how much he appreciates my mind and my values, but he would often mention that my body doesn't do me justice. That I am potentially wasting great opportunities because of my body weight. Something in the lines of nobody likes a fat person. And perhaps he was right, I don't know.

But that summer of 2013 I finally said something back. I was driving him home and it was raining like crazy. As we arrived, he decided to wait a few minutes in the car for the rain to cool off. Before that night I hadn't seen him in almost a year, so my 220 pounds caught him off guard. His honesty couldn't let go of this one I guess. All I could think was… here it comes again. And it did. All that brilliant advice that only a best friend could give. A best friend who doesn't get your pain or the daily abuse you go through. A best friend who doesn't know how much you hate yourself. This time I said something back. This time I wouldn't shut up and have someone think less of me because of my weight. I stood up for myself. I told him that my weight doesn't define me and whoever has a problem with that is not welcome in my life anyway. Nobody said it out loud but we both thought this: are you with me or against me?

Time is the best judge of everything. Don't stress yourself with questions which you are not ready to have answered. When in doubt listen to your instincts. There will be times when you need to stand up for yourself. You have to see your true value and claim the respect you deserve. Don't worry about hurting anybody's feelings, you got hurt the most already. Despite my 'I don't care attitude', my inside was broken into a zillion pieces. At this point I was definitely lost and felt as if my will, motivation and desire to live a happy life had left me completely. If I say to you I was looking into fitness and nutrition or ways to lose weight I'd be lying. I was crying and feeling sorry for myself. I was cursing and blaming my family's bad eating habits and their ignorance. I was hiding inside the house and only got out if necessary. And when out, because of the hot weather, I was sweating tremendously. The heat would make me so tired and sticky and irritable. My depression was getting worse and I had absolutely no plan on how to defeat all that.

Back then I couldn't see things as clear as I do now. After finishing my undergraduate degree in the UK, I flew back to my home country and thought that I wanted to settle there. After a few weeks it became pretty clear to me that I made the wrong choice. After so many years abroad I wasn't fitting in anymore. My old friends had made new friends, they had jobs, new relationships, I wasn't part of their life anymore. I felt like an alien. But mostly I felt alone. That realisation that I got it wrong and I didn't actually want to be there was only enhancing my depression and anxiety. It actually led to health problems and for a good few weeks I would spend my days in and out of hospital.

The reason why I wasn't looking for ways to lose weight is because my life was a mess. Nothing was settling as expected. I was back in my parents' house, unemployed and waiting for my weekly allowance. The job search was not going great at all and I was pretty much having panic attacks on a daily basis. All this uncertainty, frustration and regret that I didn't stay in the UK to seek an independent life was getting to me.

But soon things were to change.

It all started with an allergic reaction. I got home late in the evening and there was a power cut. In my country power cuts can last hours. There was nobody home so I didn't bother to enter the house. The dark freaks me out. I called some friends and met them for a drink. I was dragging the night and I wasn't myself. All I wanted was to be in bed and watch TV. It felt so forced to be out but I didn't have much of a choice. Unlike high school when crashing at a friend's place was routine, now they all had lovers and fiancées so I couldn't disturb anybody. Since I was out and had to kill time, we played some social games. I had an orange smoothie because I was driving. My friends, however, decided to go hard on alcohol.

Before I knew it we ended up in a club. An underground kind of place which was scary and super crowded. They were all intoxicated and screaming and jumping around. At some point shattered glass reached my legs. As I look up a bloke smashes a bottle on another bloke's head. I knew it was time to go home. With or without electricity in the house, it was time to make a move. As I was heading to the car I started feeling a burning sensation on my face. Instantly I thought it was an allergic reaction so I took an anti-histamine. I always used to have those pills with me. Whenever an insect bites me I get huge red spots on my skin so I would take an anti-histamine to speed up the healing time. I got in the car and I drove home. I had about ten panic attacks on the way. I was scared something worse could happen. Lucky for me the power was on and I entered the house. But I was restless. I finally called a friend and asked her if I could sleep at hers. I took my chances because she lived with her fiancée, but he was away for a few days. I drove there like a mad thing. I was afraid to be alone. What if I stop breathing? What if the burning sensation gets worse? What is happening to me?

When I finally got there Laura, my friend, who was a med student panicked even more. My tongue was swollen and white. Her wider knowledge together with our anxiety peaked while driving to A&E. The medical system in my home country is not the best or the most effective, so after five hours of waiting they finally saw me. They ran some tests and did some checking but they couldn't identify the cause of my allergy. I spent the whole night in a chair with a tube attached to my arm. It was really cold and uncomfortable. I got home at 8 am. It was a horrible experience.

The following days I had to return to the hospital and be assessed by a doctor. More tests followed and I received treatment for one month. I had to take ten anti-histamines per day. I didn't know in that moment how much my life would change. How I would finally find my path and unleash my true potential. As part of the investigation and recovery, I had to follow a strict diet for one month. Now, the doctor didn't say I couldn't have deep fried chicken, but I thought since I was restricted on what I could eat I might as well eat healthier. So I did. Something funny happens when your health is in danger. Food doesn't seem to go first anymore. I had to choose between the two, and my health won.

When I was a teenager I used to take private tennis lessons. I have always been in love with this sport but I wouldn't play much while I was studying in the UK. I was too ashamed to approach other students who were playing tennis or join any student societies. But now that I was back home I could play with my friends. My highly competitive friends. Because the weather is really lovely in summer we used to go about three times per week. If there is one sport which burns calories, trust me, it's tennis. The strength, the speed, the cardio, the resistance, all your abilities are tested throughout a game.

In that one month of treatment and healthy eating, combined with the long tennis sessions, I lost two dress sizes. Wow! I couldn't believe it! I hadn't had that body shape in years. Even when I went for my final check-up, the doctor mentioned that I had lost weight and I looked great. And I was feeling great! Suddenly my energy levels were up again and my appetite for life was back. My confidence was slowly coming back and overall I was feeling strong again. After that one month I kept on going. Why would I stop when I was feeling at my best? Food didn't matter anymore. I was on a different mission now. To feel great again and finally take care of myself.

I always thought that losing weight is about the number on the scale. I thought it was about punishing myself and inflicting more pain on my mind and body. After 100 diets I realised that losing weight is not about that at all. It is not a race that I must win. It is not about the fat percentage. It is not about cravings. Losing weight is about loving yourself again. It's about discipline, commitment and the persistence to achieve your goal.

It was finally a journey and not a race anymore. It was a healing process, not a punishment. I didn't check my weight for two months and a half. Not even once. Because I didn't care. I wasn't going to impose deadlines on myself anymore and I wasn't going to cry for not losing weight according to my crazy schedule. I wasn't going to give up, no matter what. The first few weeks, until I started to feel the benefits of the change, were challenging. I had to control my cravings, get into a new routine and learn how to eat healthier. It was quite a lot to cope with. I was asking myself the typical questions, what if? when? how? for how long? My head was spinning.

Somehow, I felt that this time was going to be different. I had never felt like that before, simply because losing weight became secondary to my purpose. Instead of waking up and thinking how many grams I had lost overnight, I would wake up thinking what new things I could try today. Things I haven't been able to do in a long time because of my extra weight. For example, go to the beach. I love being lazy in the sun and I especially love the sea. I was too ashamed to expose my body in a swimsuit and for that reason I hadn't been on a holiday in ages. Well, in that summer of 2013 I bought myself the most beautiful bathing suit I ever had and I went on a short holiday. Taking my clothes off at the beach felt overwhelming and at the same time felt great. I overcame my fear of publicly exposing my body.

That holiday was amazing for so many reasons. Firstly, I overcame many of my past fears. Secondly, I did so many activities and I had so much fun. I had the energy and desire to explore fun things and I didn't find excuses not to. Thirdly, it was the first time I did any kind of physical activity during a holiday. I played tennis three out of the four days I was there. And finally I was able to eat healthily throughout my holiday. And it didn't feel like I was losing out on anything for one second. All these changes felt natural, like that was truly part of me, the new me. When eating healthy you fear the temptation around the holiday and festive season. That's because you are just starting your journey. Once you get results and notice the benefits of a healthy, happy life you'd be surprised to find out that you don't actually crave any foods. Breaking the food addiction means many things and one of them is this: you realise that gatherings and holidays are not about food. It is not the food which makes the season great, but the quality of the time you spend with your family. Think of your last holiday for one minute. What do you remember? I'll help you. How horrible you looked in those bloody pictures and how tired and unhappy you felt the whole holiday. Did you spend quality time with your dear ones? No, because you were too ashamed of your body to actually engage in fun activities. Secondly, since food is so important in your life, do you even remember what you ate? Did your love for food save your holiday and give you brilliant memories? Of course not. Next time, when you believe food is the most important thing, take a step back and remind yourself what actually builds the lovely memories.

Confession time. I did have two glasses of wine during my holiday. But I was able to control my drinking for the first time since my teen years. Being aware of my number of drinks and taking only positive actions for my body was something new to me. I was scared and excited about these changes and I did wonder if something could happen that would make me return to my previous sad life. However, I wasn't worried about gaining the weight back this time. I was worried about the aftermath of being obese again and how that would prevent me from living this beautiful life full of adventures and fun. My worry now was rooted in losing all that appetite and love for life which I haven't had in over a decade. I felt so alive and I could have taken on any challenge life threw at me. As I am writing now I realise that nothing could have stopped me at that moment, but due to low confidence and a past full of failures I didn't acknowledge my inner strength and commitment back then.

As time passed I did lose considerable weight. I dropped four sizes within three months. I was happy with my overall progress and I felt more empowered than ever. Soon after my change happened I had a chat with Mom. She wanted to know how I was doing, coping with moving back home, how the job search was going, all the details. Despite my efforts I could never lie to Mum. She immediately knew something was wrong. I told her about my failure to adapt back home and how everything is so different and I felt like an outsider. She suggested to do some research and see if I could return for a master's degree. Blimey, I thought! My mum is giving me a second chance to choose better. Yes, I will take it! The deadline was still one month away so I had plenty of time to submit my application. I actually sent everything through whilst I was on my mini holiday. My whole life was falling into place again. I could deal with every aspect of my life and not be too tired or depressed to actually take action.

The new me was decisive, I knew what I wanted to do and I wasn't afraid anymore. I had the energy and desire to fight for a happier life. Once you feel the benefits of your change, it will become permanent.

Achieving what you have always wanted and even more is more important than any favourite foods or parties. You will be able to replace your food addiction with a constructive addiction.

Looking back I realise how much time I wasted fearing. Fear of action, fear to believe, fear to achieve my potential. I thought I wanted to lose weight but I never actually took active steps towards that. I never took the time to understand how the body works, what to eat, when to eat it, and I started watch YouTube videos of people who have succeeded to try to find a role model. I would stand in front of my mirror crying that life is unfair and blaming my parents for my uncontrollable appetite and my current body weight. When you don't actively seek change in your life it means you are not ready. It means you don't really want it.

We all know the saying 'knowledge is power'. I only agree to a certain extent. Let me explain. At this point you don't have the knowledge. By the time you finish the book you will possess a better deal of knowledge and have the tools to change your life. Now it depends on you if you are going to implement my advice or keep on leading a sad life. Thus knowledge is potential power. It can open your eyes to a deeper understanding, but what you do with it is completely your choice.

Listen to your body, mind and soul. You need all these three aligned in order to succeed. If one is not ready for change, take your time to understand why. What is truly holding you back? Life and choice are not random. There is always an underlying reason for what we do. Good or bad that reason leads the way, so you must find it. And if it is negative make it positive. Think of a glass as half full. The positive you is grateful for the full half. The negative you complains that the glass is half empty. And after you become a mum it all becomes even more challenging. Your child can be your reason to be better every day or your excuse to give up on a happy life. The baby is not making the choice, you are.

This time my reason was positive. I didn't see training or healthy eating as the punishment necessary to achieve my dream body. I saw it all as an amazing journey and I was blessed to have discovered my path and get better each day. My burning desire to get my dream body presented me with a greater opportunity. It showed me the way to inner peace and self-love.

When I checked my weight after two months and a half I had lost fifty-five pounds. I was like what? I hadn't been that weight since high school. And yet something funny happened. I was kind of upset I didn't lose more although I had no deadline or weight goal previously established. It was my old habit kicking in. That old habit where the number on the scale could change my emotions and make me doubt my progress. It took my emotions a few days to settle and I was so disappointed in myself. Unlike before, I didn't think of giving up and overeating again. This episode however made me realise the power of the scale. When you struggle your whole life with weight issues your happiness becomes dependent on a number. When all the abuse and the jokes are because of your body weight, that number takes charge of your emotions. And there is nothing more depressing that the thought that you have no value whatsoever. That number doesn't make you more or less precious, and it doesn't add or remove values and principles in your life. So next time when you check your weight, do it for fun. Don't let it control your feelings. You are in charge of your body and weight, not the other way around.

From that point onwards my weight loss slowed down. I reached the point I feared. If I don't lose weight fast enough am I going to eat again? Many fair attempts have been made before, and the minute I would reach a plateau or lose very little weight I would get extremely frustrated and return to the old habits. Remember how this time I was on a journey and it wasn't a race anymore? The speed of the process didn't matter, I had complete trust in what I was doing. Trust got me going. When you doubt yourself because of your past experiences, anchor your emotions into something you trust. That way you will keep going. I had lost the rest of my thirty-five pounds over the next nine months or so. It was so slow that I wasn't even sure I was losing weight at all. Throughout this period I didn't own a set of scales anymore. I would check my weight at the gym no more than once per month.

And that's how I discovered another secret which helped me to keep going. The power of visual. I took progress pictures on the first of every month. I would do collage on my laptop and compare the current pictures with the previous ones. And maybe month on month the difference was not huge, but let's say every three months the difference was massive. Watching those pictures again and again gave me the confidence that I was doing the right thing. That my approach this time was sustainable and indeed providing amazing results. I remember the first time I bought myself proper gym leggings and a tight fitness top. I went to the store and I got it without trying it on. I knew that if I had tried it on I would not buy it. I could feel my reluctance to wear anything like that. Was I looking good enough to leave the saggy clothes behind me? Despite my great progress and building some confidence in the whole journey, every time I would attempt something new I felt scared. It could have been clothes or an activity, but I was doubting myself. Did I have enough confidence to wear this or do this? What if I look ridiculous? What if I can't finish what I start?

By this time I was looking decent and I had only about fifteen pounds to lose to reach my goal weight. In my head however I was not ready to expose my body to criticism. I definitely had more confidence now than ever before. The problem was that the painful memories of bullying kept resurfacing and I was afraid of dragging any attention on me. I knew those tight clothes would get some attention and I wasn't sure I wanted to be wearing them. I came home and I tried my new outfit on. I stared at myself in the mirror for over thirty minutes. I actually thought I was looking OKish. 'I can wear this at the gym,' I said to myself. I was however seeking further confirmation. So I made the house my catwalk and visited all my housemates to get an opinion. Their feedback was positive and they assured me I would not look ridiculous wearing the outfit outside the house. I trusted them and stepped out. I felt a bit shy and exposed, but as nobody called me any names I got more comfortable and confident.

At this point I was back in the UK for my master's degree and I had just moved in with my new fellow student housemates. When I reached my heaviest weight, 220 pounds, I was in the UK studying as an undergraduate. Returning to the town that got me obese woke up many fears. Actually, I remember before leaving my home town one of my friends said, 'Don't get fat again in England, OK?' I feared the hectic student life would push me back into bad habits. Takeaways, partying, drinking, random sleeping schedule, and evidently no training at all. Would I still eat healthily? Can I stick to my new eating habits? The first thing I did after finding accommodation was get a gym membership and I went for my first gym session before finishing unpacking my stuff. I went to the supermarket and I got all the greens, fruits and lean meat you can think of. I did not feel tempted by the chocolate cheesecake, the blueberry muffin or the bacon sandwich. I had to be this precise because these used to be my favourites and I would literally have boxes of them every day. Being in the shop and not have my cravings wake up was a huge step forward. Events like this at first sight mean nothing, but for me it was a victory. Not only did I not have to control my craving, the craving was gone all together. When the change is permanent you will be amazed at yourself. The only way to find out where you are at in your journey is by seeking exposure to confront your fears.

Action cures fear. I could have locked myself in the house and been afraid to meet anybody. I could have ordered my food online and never set foot in a store. But is that really the way to live? Don't forget that my weight loss journey turned up to be a healing process. As such, I was now seeking to live a happy life, in fulfillment and achievement. Isolating myself socially and always wondering 'what if' would not have provided me with the life I had waited to have for twenty-two years. I now had more friends and acquaintances than ever before. I was finally loving going out and I would use every occasion to overdress. My whole life I wanted to wear high heels and tight dresses and actually look smoking hot in them. It was my turn to shine, baby. In a few months I purchased dozens of dresses, the most I have ever had. My long-awaited dream came true. Those outfits would make me feel feminine, confident, empowered.

When I was doing my degree I barely opened my mouth in class. I was extremely embarrassed of my body and I didn't want to attract more attention. Unless asked something, I used to sit in the back and wait for the class to end. I did love what I studied in uni and sometimes I regret I didn't get more involved in the whole degree/student life. But how could I have done it when my life was a mess? When you hate living inside your body when you don't see any value in yourself, how on earth can you grow? It wasn't long after arriving in the UK that my depressive symptoms enhanced. The weather, the inability to fit in, the embarrassment to approach people, my permanent worry that my accent was too strong, this whole new environment felt too much. My dream to study abroad soon became a nightmare. My relationship with my housemates slowly deteriorated, the friends I had made soon betrayed me, and despite enjoying my course I didn't excel due to my inability to focus. As my depression got worse, I gained more and more weight. I went from 160 to 220 pounds in three years.

When I came back for my master's degree in September 2013, I felt like a new person. It was the same town and uni, but somehow it was all different. This time I was in control. This time I was ready to conquer. I still enjoyed the night life but my drinking was calculated and I wasn't blacking out anymore. Most times I wouldn't drink alcohol at all, I'd have water and juice. And surprisingly I had the same amount of fun – without the hangover of course. I am living proof that it is fully your choice how you want to live. Don't waste your time and energy blaming the environment, the people around you, the temptations. Take charge of your life and control your habits. It doesn't matter where you are geographically. There are healthy foods and water wherever you might travel or live. There are friends who have a good influence in your life and others who don't. It is your job to choose the right people around you and make sure you stay on your path.

Having control over your habits, body and emotions will give you the power to control every single aspect of your life. You will become disciplined and organized and doing stuff will seem easier than procrastinating for days or weeks. You will have the energy TO DO! As an undergraduate I never thought I would obtain my diploma. I didn't care much about my academic success and I wasn't putting much work in. I remember I had a seminar at 9 am on a Wednesday. It was way too early for me, so I used to keep breaking my own snake record. For those who don't know, snake was an amazing game which used to be on mobile phones before all the smartphone madness started. Anyway, I swear it was as if my brain would switch off automatically. I couldn't focus at all and my tiredness and weakness utterly took me over. I soon gave up on attending that seminar, it was pure torture for a depressed person to make it in time. Finishing my coursework before the deadline was indeed my greatest challenge. Although I knew months in advance I had work to submit, I was never able to plan my to-do list accordingly. Most times the start and end day of a set of coursework was the night before the deadline. I was highly irresponsible but it never felt that way. In my head I was trying my best and it wasn't my fault nothing was working out. Looking back I was the only one responsible for my life and choices. More weight I had gained and more depressed I had become.

Human beings are way too complex, so if there is one element not functioning properly it affects all aspects of the existence. I was overeating because of my inner pain. My overeating made me obese. My obesity made me depressed. My depression almost ruined my life. It was all a crazy toxic cycle that never seemed to end. I had to take charge and end it. I had to stand up for myself and claim my life back. It all starts with small changes and a burning desire to be happier.

Summary

When your 'aha' moment comes don't let go of it. Don't bury it as if it was never there. Change is super hard but trust me, living in pain and frustration is 100 times harder. Once the change becomes permanent and you enjoy the benefits of your new life you will feel liberated. It takes a little bit of discipline for a life full of love and joy. How much is your life worth?

No doctor has been able to identify the cause of my allergy. I now think that allergy was given to me as a chance to change my life. If it wasn't for the doctor's eating plan I would have carried on with my old habits. But I listened to my body and I had my aha moment. It was now or never. And I chose NOW! If I were to go back in time a million times I would make exactly the same choices. I learnt so many lessons throughout my life and the only reason why I am truly amazing today is because of my past. Don't let your past experience be your handicap and don't fear action. The trial and error of the past were all designed to bring you here. Each failure was meant to teach you something, a much greater understanding than your inability to progress into your journey. Only time will reveal why certain things happened in a particular way. Your duty is to accept them and move on.

Chapter 4
Body acceptance

I was obese until the age of twenty-two.

For twenty-two years I was seeking only one answer:
why am I obese?

As a child I remember not fitting into many clothes.
The trendy outfits were never a good match for my
fluffy body. Short skirts, crop tops, wedges, tight
jeans, I couldn't wear any of these things. I don't
know if I looked horrible in clothes such as these at
that age, but I sure know my parents would have
never let me wear anything like that. They used to
say that my body shape and weight would not look
very pleasant in certain outfits and I should never
attempt wearing anything like that outside the house.
My abuser, my father, was convinced people would
laugh at me and he had no reluctance whatsoever to
share those thoughts with me, a child.

I would always wear three quarter or long trousers
and because of my thick thighs they would always
get ripped in between my legs. All my pairs were well
patched in order to resist the friction. I was truly
embarrassed by the extra tailoring my clothes needed
in order to last longer. And every time I would dare
to wear a skirt, I would end up with a rash or

sometimes an actual wound in between my thighs. Most of the time I had to cut a pair of tights in half and wear them underneath the skirt. I didn't want to wear the full tights because it was super hot in summer, anywhere between 25–35 celsius. The actual reason why I didn't feel comfortable wearing the whole tights is because I was ashamed that somebody would notice and bully me.

It was extremely painful for me to accept that reality and I always found ways to cover myself. I was ashamed of my body and the clothes I had to wear. And the worst part was that my family was completely supporting that lack of love and confidence I was experiencing. No surprise that as a teenager I ended up hating everything about my body and I was wearing the most horrible, saggy, dark clothes in order to cover the rolls of fat. Once the abuse and the bullying happens within the family it is impossible to escape it. All you can do is build coping mechanisms. As a child I wasn't allowed to wear tight clothes, as a teenager my clothes were too saggy. I was never able to satisfy the requirements or expectations of my family. I was confused and I couldn't understand what was expected of me. Since my desperate attempts to do things right had all failed I developed bad coping mechanisms, such as overeating and overdrinking.

I often wonder what it would have been like to have a family who actually accepted my body the way it was. What it would have been like not to be the subject of all jokes.

I love my brothers like crazy but they were proper arseholes. From careful where you sit in the car so we don't flip over on the road, to are you going to eat the plate as well as your lunch, their jokes were too much. That's the thing. Because emotional and psychological abuse can easily be disguised into jokes which have a positive meaning, you don't even know when to get offended and when not to. Oh, I guess the most recurrent joke was… nobody is ever going to marry you because you are fat. Or worse, someone will marry you but he will cheat on you.

I had no choice but laugh at all this. As a victim of bullying the worst thing to do is to voice out your pain. Once the soft spot is identified the abuse will keep coming.

At that point in my life I didn't even dare to think about body acceptance. What is there about my body to be liked? Or for that matter in myself as a human being? I had an uncle and aunty living five hours away from my hometown. Each and every one of their visits would end up in me getting extremely hurt and humiliated. It's so frustrating when unhealthy, obese people try and educate you on weight issues. It starts with 'now I know I am not the fittest but I'm fifty. You are young and you have your whole life ahead of you'. I bloody hate this line, and if I ever use it I hope lightning strikes me.

Because of the toxic environment I grew up in I never liked my body. I hated every inch of it. First it was my weight. Then it extended to my nose, my skin colour, my hairy arms, my breasts and the list goes on. As a teenager all I ever wanted was to love myself and feel loved by others. I always felt I could do more or be better, but I never actually reached my full potential back then. My lack of confidence prevented me from growing out of my misery and doing extraordinary things. I wanted to feel alive, be happy, and achieve whatever crazy goals I had. I didn't feel much love as a teenager and I was craving it so badly. I wanted to feel appreciated for who I was. I had my best friend back then, Denise. She was so amazing and sensitive. She's like a kitten who loves hugs and cuddles. Denise made my teenage years much easier and I wouldn't have kept my sanity without her. It's funny how quick we judge others. We used to go to the same school, but I couldn't stand her. Years later, after we became classmates, we built a tremendous friendship. We used to always go shopping together. As I was trying on clothes Denise could see sadness kicking in because nothing I liked fit me. She would tell me how I looked pretty anyway and would kiss my cheek. She gave me love in the darkest time of my teenage years. She appreciated me and stood by my side. Thank you, Denise. I will forever be grateful for your care, love and good heart.

After so many years of abuse it was my conviction that by losing weight all my self-esteem and body acceptance issues would be sorted. After twenty-two years of obesity I found my path and I lost all the extra weight. I lost ninety pounds in roughly one year and a half. What I discovered as I was losing the weight is that I couldn't ignore my pain anymore. I could feel the inner power and confidence given by the healthy lifestyle, but at the same time it felt as if something was holding me back, not allowing me to truly discover myself. I was still a wounded young girl trying to find herself. Only after I started working on my inner pain and objectively analysed my life did I start to see myself as a new person. I learnt a tremendous lesson here. Sometimes it is not even about your body. Your insecurity and low confidence has deeper roots and unless you find them and work out your inner issues, losing weight alone will not heal you. You will enjoy a short life span of enjoyment without any actual healing.

I have a funny friend who told me something very interesting on a random day: 'you will always have a little fat girl inside you'. I laughed. I said to him to stop envying my new body shape. It took me a long time to understand what he meant. He wasn't talking about my cravings or my fear to slide back into bad habits. He was talking about my insecurities and inability to love my body. Fat or skinny, it took a great deal to love my body. If it wasn't a high fat percentage it was stretch marks. If it wasn't stretch marks it was loose skin or saggy breasts. I was never, ever satisfied. The trauma was too deep and I was scared to rise above my fear.

And then I became a mom. After a few months of extreme hate towards my body, something magical happened. I actually started to love my mommy body. All the marks and permanent pregnancy changes were there to remind me what a fantastic job I did. Once I stopped living a selfish, self-absorbed life and my baby became my life the looks of my body didn't matter anymore. I suddenly realised that my body doesn't really define me as a person. It is my temple and I need to take care of it in order to be healthy and fit and strong enough to care for my son, but it doesn't have to be perfect. My loose skin doesn't make me a bad mom or unworthy.

Life taught me that my body is the tool that gets everything done. My ability to fulfill my daily goals and chores depends on the care I invest in my body. I am not talking about moisturising my skin every day, but about what I actually eat and how I maintain my stamina and resistance. An overloaded and sedentary body will never perform well. When you eat unhealthy foods your digestion becomes heavier. Your digestive system will have to work harder and longer to pass through the foods. That means that your body will invest more energy into that process and make you tired sooner. Instead of preserving that energy or making it into something productive, you end up getting tired because you ate too much.

Body acceptance is not about being obese or complacent. Body acceptance is not about giving up on your ability to make smarter choices. Body acceptance should be about your understanding that your stretch marks don't define you, that the width of your hips don't make you less valuable. How far should body acceptance go? There is a lot of controversy around this topic and I am afraid that society got it wrong again. Instead of finding the right balance to live by, the concept has evidently been taken to the other extreme. Since becoming a mom I completely militate for body acceptance. If you don't love yourself who will? However, what I completely dislike is using body acceptance as a platform to promote obesity and a unhealthy lifestyle overall.

Mostly likely you will be outraged by my statement. It's not your fault. A size twenty-six model cannot, should not, must not, be promoted as a role model for body acceptance. The chances of diabetes, heart disease, stroke, cancer, liver failure are greatly increased. And then let's talk about her personal discomfort. She is restricted from taking the stairs or using tubes at an aqua park and has to use two seats on a plane. I read this online. Sometimes obese people even buy their own seat belt extension because they feel ashamed and bullied by the airline staff. Is that really what body acceptance is about? Because if it is, then I am against it.

I will never believe that a size twenty-six person is happy and loves her curves. In my head she is not able to play with her kids, wear the clothes that she likes, walk long distances, go shopping or take care of herself. Sex is not crazy either, because she doesn't have the stamina to enjoy long sessions. Or complicated twists for that matter. I know what it is like to be obese as a young woman. I know what it is like to be obese as a mother. I don't like lies and I don't believe the BS a size twenty-six model tries to sell. Whatever story you tell yourself every day in order to accept the extra weight, all you are doing is deceiving yourself.

If you are not obese yet, well, I was – twice. Size eighteen to twenty. I was miserable. It was the darkest time of my life. But I took responsibility for my chaotic eating and lack of movement and I never used body acceptance as an excuse for my failure to make better choices for myself. As I mentioned above, having my family as the main abuser didn't do much for my confidence. However, when your body is fighting hard to finish the day, how can you feel self-love then? At my heaviest I felt as if I was disabled. I couldn't take the stairs, put shoes on without all the blood going to my head, shave my legs, play any kind of sports where I had to run or even walk. It was hard even to play with my baby nephew. Was I really living the dream life? At that point in my life food was no longer making me happy. It was an addiction and I didn't know how to stop. I wanted it to stop but I was so scared of trying and failing that I would give in all together. What is worse than not loving your body is hating yourself for being weak and scared.

My problem with body acceptance started recently after I read an article stuff online. It seems that encouraging people to get fit and regain control over their eating habits and exercise is highly offensive.

You are considered a bully for wanting to add years to their lives. However, encouraging people to do something about their depressed life and tired bodies is uplifting. What happened to the world?

The same way promoting underweight models or fully Botoxed teenagers is wrong, encouraging obesity is equally wrong. I wouldn't want my son to believe that obesity can make you happy and give you a great life, full of accomplishments and enjoyment. I wouldn't want him to give up on making smarter choices just because some person out there is selling the biggest BS on the market.

Summary

Body acceptance is about feelings and appearance. It is about living in agreement with your mind and body. It is about seeing your true value and treating your body as the tool that gets things done. Imagine your body being like your best employee. You want to keep him excited so the incentives must be good. If you want your body to perform at its best, then eat and exercise accordingly.

Learn how to love your imperfections, such as stretch marks and body shape. Don't spend a life in frustration waiting to improve something which might not even make you happier. Getting fake breasts for example seems to be a very strong trend. Imagine working for years to afford the surgery and then when it's done you don't like them. Or your body might reject the implants. Is it really worthy to sacrifice everything for an improvement which is not even necessary?

Choose your role models carefully. Aim for people who have done better and achieve great things, not for those who failed. Always aim higher and never become complacent in your pain and anger. Ask yourself this: Am I capable of making smarter choices?

Role models are supposed to change as you evolve in life. As a teenager you might choose a singer, as a young woman an influencer, as a mom a blogger and as a professional a successful business idol. Depending on your priorities, your idols will get replaced. What matters is to always aim higher and never give in to your pain.

Chapter 5

It took me 100 diets

Weight loss is a huge deal these days. Everybody is talking about it. Studies have proven that many diseases can be avoided, even in old age, if you take care of your body. If you are unlucky and do have some sort of illness, a clean lifestyle would reduce your need of medication and thus increase life expectancy. That's the reason why everybody talks about weight loss. Despite a general acceptance that obesity is causing many health issues and mental disorders, more and more people seem to be overweight.

Despite endless healthy choices on the market, and all the organic and least processed food you can think of being literally available everywhere, you find yourself making the most unhealthy choices. Your lack of confidence in making smarter choices seems to get worse by the day. And yet it looks like the world is more ready than ever to lose weight and be fit and healthy. From TV shows to documentaries, from structured workouts to free trials, society seems to acknowledge the importance of being fit and looking great.

Pop stars, actresses, TV moderators, they all emphasise on how healthy they live and the sacrifices they make to look amazing. Not only are they are on the craziest, most restrictive diets, but most of them hire the most well-known personal trainers to sculpture their bodies. And when that is not enough there is always artificial beauty, from Botox to liposuction and other crazy pain inflicting procedures.

The world is ready to create the perfect body. Naturally or with a little bit of help, your dream body can be achieved. And with that being the case, why are you still overweight? What's stopping you from losing the weight and looking at your best? Because the extra weight most of the time is the result of a hectic life. A life which controls you. Being overweight in this day and age, when access to healthy eating and workouts is free and everywhere, means the issue is deeper.

It took me 100 diets to discover the secret of a balanced life. It took me 100 diets to love myself. It took me 100 diets to finally treat my body right.

My whole life I had weight issues. As a child I was overweight, as a teenager fat, and as a young woman in my early twenties, obese. My extra weight has always been my number one enemy. Everything that would go wrong in my life, in my head, was because of my body. I couldn't have loving, caring friends because I wasn't worthy of love. I couldn't have a peaceful relationship because of my insecurity issues, which would make me super jealous. And finally my close and extended family would bully me on a daily basis. There was a lot of pain to take in and all because of my extra weight. I hated my body vehemently and eventually I did get to the point where I was fully depressed and on the verge of giving up.

As I grew up the hate towards myself and my body intensified. The feeling of being worthless intensified. Ironically, I never thought of actually getting angry at my environment. I was overweight, I was different, I deserved the daily psychological abuses. It was my fault that I couldn't fit in. When I was five years old I visited my grandma in the village. Since Grandma didn't have a car, the only way to get some sweets was an hour's walk to the shop. I was definitely not willing to do that. Grandma was way too busy to bake me something, so the only option I had was sugar on bread. For me it was the best dessert. I literally took a spoon of sugar and dropped it on a slice of bread. And Grandma saw me and told me to stop eating. She said I was too fat to have sweets and that I was different and I had to be more careful. Grandma was supposed to spoil the shit out of me and yet all I got was further abuse. I cried the whole day. It made me feel rejected. I often reminisce and wonder if these adults ever wondered what I was going through. I could never do that to my nephews or my child. They mean the world to me and their bodies or life choices don't make them less valuable. So how could they do that to me? I still wonder at times why they would hurt me to that extent.

I started developing the shame and guilt of overeating at the age of nine. If you ask me it was a bit too early to become self-conscious of my body. Every bite I had added to my guilt, to my feeling of worthlessness for not being able to control myself. How could I have controlled myself when food was my escape from the pain inflicted by the people who were supposed to love me the most?

While I was on this diet my family's eating habits never changed. I would eat tomato salad while they were having doughnuts. I would eat soup while the steaks and fries were coming off their plates. My mum was the only one who would diet with me. Honestly, I appreciated her effort, but deep down I wish she'd never taken me for that appointment and made me go through all that pain. I was supposed to understand I was fat and different and for that reason I wasn't allowed to eat like everybody else.

Nobody ever wondered if the eating habits in the house should change. This one time they were supposed to lead by example. Adults need to stop underestimating children. They are literally a sponge, ready to absorb it all. I never said it out loud evidently, but I used to think why can they eat the forbidden foods and I'm not allowed to? I mean look at them, they are so fat they can't even put their shoes on. In my family everybody is still overweight to morbidly obese. And yet I have always been the only one who needed to change, because I am a girl and as a girl I have to be small and gentle. Otherwise society will bully me and nobody will marry me. Hello, my dear family, in your attempt to protect me from the outside world you abused me the most!

Two major things happened after this episode: my metabolism went south and my confidence vanished completely and permanently. From that point onwards I would put all my efforts into getting the dream body. Brilliant choice you might think. The problem was that my means of doing it were completely wrong. When you don't love yourself and you react based on negative feelings and thoughts, your actions are very likely to be self-destructive. The pain is choking you and you want a quick fix. And you would do anything to discover that magic formula that will shed off the extra weight and bring self-love back into your life.

I want to summarise the stupid mistakes I made: starvation, forcing myself to vomit, laxatives, no carbs diets, extremely low calorie diet, replacing food with water, and many others. Some of these methods did help me lose weight. I mean, when you eat an apple a day, of course, some weight will fall off. But it was not sustainable. Before I knew it I was back on ground zero, overeating in my room and crying because I was incapable to commit to a better life. When you try to lose weight by using extreme, unhealthy measures, there is no maintenance diet after that. You never get there. First you give up before losing the weight you desire, and secondly you have got no nutritional plan in place to ensure maintenance.

After years of bullying and psychological abuse I was damaged. Trying to get my dream body whilst my inner pain was still active didn't work out very well. Every few weeks I would start a new diet. No carbs, no eating after
6 pm, no meat, hot water with lemon, you name it, I have done it all. So many times I would have just a glass of water for dinner. I starved myself a lot. My last starvation mode ended up pretty badly. After three weeks of living on fruit I fainted and woke up in A&E.

When starvation wouldn't work anymore I would overeat and force myself to puke. That was nasty, trust me. One of the most horrible things I have done to myself. I particularly remember one evening. My brothers and I were having a barbecue. We spent the whole day getting everything ready, from meat to salad and snacks. The food was amazing and the party was going great. After I was done stuffing my face I locked myself in the bathroom and spent the next thirty minutes puking. In retrospect, I didn't do that to lose weight, it was punishment. It was my punishment for enjoying the party. How can an unworthy person like me have a good time?

The reason why I didn't do it the right way is not because I didn't know how to necessarily, or that I wanted quick results. I chose hardcore ways of losing weight because I had to punish myself for my extra weight. I had to suffer in this process of changing my body. And that's exactly the reason why you have failed before too. Your pain is manipulating you into making the worst decisions for weight loss. With free, instant access to all kinds of information, nutrition, diets, blogs on how to, there is no excuse to still be obese. Unless the inner you is too damaged to take the lead and guide you into a beautiful life. Wanting to be better, look better, and grow as a person is a natural desire for most people. Some want to be healthier, some become vegetarians, some get a better job, some do volunteering. Regardless, every action you take should be gentle on you and bring you one step closer to happiness. My lack of love and appreciation for my own person made me my worst enemy. The extent to which I would constantly judge myself, punish myself, put myself down, I don't think I could ever do it to somebody else.

I remember waking up in the morning and looking into the mirror I had in my room. I would turn from all angles and maybe, maybe, I'd find an inch of my body that I liked. That never happened. I look at pictures from then and realise how distorted I was. I was not even that fat. I didn't have the ideal weight but I was a girl able to do whatever she wanted. My weight was not interfering with my daily activities yet. It seems that it was literally just the looks of my body that highly disturbed everybody around me. And it makes me think how selfish they were. They used their own frustration to hurt me. Because they couldn't do any better, I had to take the hit for their unachievement. The reflection of my body in that mirror is a memory which will stay with me forever. I used to grab my stomach and pull it. I wished I could cut it and make it disappear instantly. And I would cry so much. I would feel this heavy pain in my chest and an enormous level of anger. I would scream at myself as a reminder that I am useless, that

I can't lose weight and be 'normal'. I was imagining how good my life could be if only I were skinny. How all the psychological abuse would vanish and I could finally be loved and appreciated.

I truly believed back then that being skinny meant complete happiness. Skinny women must be living the dream: having lots of friends, men who appreciate them and a family who respects them. You see, I didn't have that. But let me tell you something. Your body weight, shape, colour, height, whatever you hate of yourself right now, is not the cause of your pain. As a human being you deserve better treatment and if you are not getting that it is because you allow them to inflict emotional and psychological torture on you. You are the reason why they do it. Using my body, my bullies managed to make me doubt my true self, my value, my right to live a happy life. I was abused to the point where it became my conviction that my body equals shame, punishment, worthlessness, an endless list of negative feelings.

And it was this conviction amongst other negative ones, that made me do everything wrong. When you have no love for your body or yourself, every action you take will be damaging. I often think of my struggle to lose weight. I like to analyse myself a lot, so I try and be as objective as possible. I never really cared that I could permanently endanger my health. I never cared of being moody due to low calorie diets or lack of carbs. I didn't care that I was starving myself and was weak and dizzy most of the time. I just wanted my pain to end. Funny enough, none of those destructive actions solved my problem.

It took me 100 diets and lots of self-punishment to discover the secrets of sustainable results. It wasn't food causing me the pain, but the outside world. The torture and the pain will not become numb, no matter how much or little you eat. The answer is within you. The healing journey is emotional as much as it is physical. I know, your goal is to become skinny and live the perfect life. What you don't know yet is that unless you close your wounds losing weight would not give you the dream life. It is a rigorous process and it requires lots of discipline and a strong will.

Summary

Next time you think of what you really want, set your priorities straight. Life is not a fantasy. You have been hurt because of your looks and getting the dream body will not erase all that. You need time to build up your confidence, self-esteem and love for yourself.

The pain of the past is extremely strong. Unless acknowledged, you can't move forward. Accept it and work with it. Heal your body and soul, and the next time you wonder why you failed your answer is in this chapter. The next time you are thinking to damage your health or body just to lose weight, read this chapter again. Make it your daily reading until you heal, until you get control.

I ate because it hurt. And the more it hurt, the more I ate. I ate because I was convinced that I was different and I wasn't worthy of love and appreciation. Food will never give you the emotional numbness you are truly seeking. Healing your inner self is the solution to your failure.

Chapter 6

Kill the fear

As I am writing this my cheeky one is fourteen months. And not long ago he became my role model. Every day I am amazed at his natural, pure intelligence. I can already see his temper and behavioural traits. And whilst some friends and family advise me to hinder his spirit and make him behave better, I truly believe he is brilliant. He doesn't know fear. I never used fear as a tool to educate him. The result: he is fearless. Even when he falls and gets hurt, he will stand up and try again. If he wants something, he will use all means to obtain it. And he chases dogs and birds and runs around without a care, if I am in his proximity or not. At fourteen months old he does things I am too scared to do: explore the unknown, take risks, be adventurous.

Unlike my son, I fear most of the time. What if? is my most common thought. The anxiety has made things even worse. Because of my past experiences and everything that I have been taught within the family and school, I developed many fears. Some are mine, some are borrowed from my environment. My mom developed throat cancer when I was five. I grew up watching her choke on air. Literally. A gasp of air that made her cough or was ticklish inside her throat and you could see the panic on her face. Her eyes would open wide and her forehead would start sweating. Foods, drinks, snacks, there is a whole list of stuff she hasn't touched since because of fear of suffocation. Her fear is completely unreasonable. But she made it her conviction that certain foods would kill her so she chose to fully deprive herself.

And I took some of her fears. My whole life I fought against it, but eventually it got me. I am definitely not as strong as I could be. Observing my son inspires me. Makes me stronger. It makes me realise the amazing, incredible potential we are born with and how we get all broken in the process of growing up. What a shame, I swear! So much could be achieved!

My whole life I was scared to confront my bullies. Those bullies that you can't stop seeing, like relatives, family or school friends. When I finally did, it was the best moment of my life. When I stood up for myself and told my brothers they are being d*cks and I don't appreciate their stupid jokes, silence took over the room. A very low 'didn't know you cared' finally broke the silence. Well I do, so please respect me as a human being and stop repeating how worthless I am because of my extra weight.

In school I had to beat a few of them, but they finally got it. The fatty went crazy they said. Perhaps I did, but at least I wasn't scared anymore. The only cure for fear is ACTION! Living in fear could shadow the best moments of your life. Instead of giving yourself to the moment, fully immerse yourself in that amazing experience as you sit in a corner wondering what if. And 90% of the time, what if it never happens? When recalling the event later on, there will no happy memory. What you will recollect is a terrifying memory of a danger that never happened.

There are so many reasons why you have to defeat your fears. I think the most important one is this: YOURSELF! How are you supposed to grow and become better by the day if you don't allow yourself new experiences? The only way to learn and discover is by putting yourself out there. Get out from your shell and explore! Breathe in the freedom of a life full of action. I know it sounds crazy, but defeating one fear a day will empower you. I am full of fears and wonders. My mommy anxiety seems to never get any better really. But I act against my fears and take a leap of faith. I say to myself 'keep being petrified and get nothing done or put yourself out there and cope with life.' And 90% of the time I feared for no reason. Even if it didn't go according to the plan, I defeated my fear and discovered that it is not as bad as I thought it would be.

I only acknowledged self-sabotage in my early twenties. Your mind can be your best friend or your worst enemy. It is the most powerful tool. How it works, with you or against you, is actually up to you. I have to admit I always build scenarios in my head. How a date might go, how emotions will take over during an exam, how to deliver bad news, the list is endless. Very few of them ever became reality. And even when they did, I coped. And with every fear that I overcame, I became stronger. Fear, act, understand and grow.

When I decided I'd had enough of my obese life and it was then or never, I feared so much it would be another one of those one-week diets and then give up. But this time it was different. Every day I would wake up more determined to achieve, to make smarter, healthier choices. And as time passed and I saw my progress, I knew there was no going back. I was on the right path. Little wins add up to a greater goal. Instead of getting frustrated that I reached a plateau or I am not burning fat at a desired pace, I would tell myself how great I have been doing so far and that this time it is not a race. It is a burning desire to become better and this whole journey has achieved just that. Not just physically, but emotionally and mentally. And the more you heal your inner self the easier it becomes. I slowly regained my confidence, my energy, my happiness. I was actively living a beautiful life. No more going through the day like a zombie.

Think of your own fears for a second. What happens when one of them gets activated? You have the feeling of fear, the thought of panic, the physical symptoms, heart palpitations, sweat, dilated pupils, and ultimately you are petrified. Fear is an extremely powerful deterrent. Your subconscious stores all these experiences and your survival mechanism will tell you not to do it when put in a situation where you have to face your fear.

When you feel fear you must act. Even better, put yourself in a position of fear. I am scared of bees. I got stung a few times and for those who don't know, it is very painful. So when I see a bee, even if it's outside the car, I panic. My defence mechanism kicks in and tells me to stay inside the car. I decided to defeat my fear and gradually expose myself to the external factor. In my case, the bee. First time I did it, I cried. I thought my heart would come out of my chest. But I stood there, I needed to act in order to reduce my fear. And now my subconscious registered a different reaction to bees. And slowly I kept on exposing myself. Now I can actually take my son to the park in summer without being petrified with fear every second. Amazing progress!

What do you want to change about yourself? Are you seeking to feel better, look better, be happier, more confident, and finally have control over your life? Whatever you seek to achieve, there are no limits to your capacity to commit. You must be thinking that taking a big ass decision regarding your own life is too much to handle. There is a reason why you are reading this book. It was written for those who want to be greater, make better choices, enjoy and live life at its fullest. However, you are scared. You have failed so many times before that you have given up on the life that you deserve. I want to refer here to the fears you developed over time because of the failed attempts to improve the quality of your life: fear of diets, fear of training, fear of lack of time, fear of lack of motivation, fear of bad days, fear of weight plateau, fear of not meeting your weight target, fear of not losing weight fast enough, fear of God's acts, fear of kids getting sick, fear of partner being unsupportive, fear of winter, fear of holidays, fear of weekends, fear of parties, fear of trying new clothes on, fear of watching yourself in the mirror, fear of a lack of compliments, fear of lack of accountability, fear of experiencing the guilt feeling, fear of temptation, fear of gatherings, fear of changing your routine, fear of prioritising, fear of the scales, and last but not least, fear of failing again.

I have experienced each and every one of these fears, and every failed attempt to be better ended up in a stronger belief that I cannot, will not, improve my life. The mistake you make is that you want to break all these fears at the same time. Even more, you want to break them by thinking of them and not actually facing them in real life. It doesn't work like that. Just because that one time the outcome was rubbish and your subconscious recorded it as an unpleasant experience, it doesn't mean you can't break the fear in the future.

I was terrified of the scales. Not the actual scales, but checking my weight. Whenever I would start a new diet the scales were the first factor to put me off. In my head I had stupid, mad expectations, which of course I'd never meet. And every weight check was pure mental torture. I was doing it wrong. You see, I used to check my weight every day. Every single morning I would step on the scales and excitedly expect to have lost a lot of weight overnight. I didn't know back then that there is a whole list of factors influencing your weight and checking it every day would only do two things: first, make me doubt the process, and secondly, develop a stupid addiction to the number on the scales.

Checking my weight every day has never helped me in my journey to lose weight. I remember asking myself why after putting in so much effort does the weight stay the same? And my next thought was giving up and accepting a life full of pain.

The way I found my path was different than anything I had tried before. Every time I would make the decision to lose weight, I would normally just jump on a strict diet and maybe do some exercises. This time I had a long talk with myself and wrote down the reasons why I have to succeed. I also wrote down my fears and everything that I did wrong before. The scales was in the top five. So I decided to stay away from them completely. Since the number on the scales had the power to change my emotions, I decided to stop checking my weight. Remember, if you can't control, stay away! When I eventually checked my weight, despite crazy results, I was expecting to have lost more. That number on the scales made me upset for a day or two, but this time I didn't give in, I carried on with my mission. And that's how I crushed my scales addiction.

The minute I decided to get healthier because my body was sending me all the signals to take action and change, I stopped the scales addiction. For two months and a half I did not step on the scales once. It was the most liberating feeling ever. My journey was not conditioned by the scales anymore, I could have weighed whatever as long as I was on track with my nutritional and training plan. I was finally not miserable in the process of losing weight. I knew I did everything in my power to achieve my goal, and the scales lost its power over me.

Making a change whilst still surrounded by your old, toxic environment can be quite challenging. Your friends and family will of course invite you to parties, outings, holidays and getaways and so forth. And that's great, because you love them and you want to spend time with them, however, you must always have this mind: if you can't control it, stay away! If you put yourself in the middle of temptation from the very beginning of your journey, you will likely give in. Until your skills to control your cravings are well developed, until you see the benefits of a healthier life, until you actually feel much better about yourself, you are vulnerable. It won't be this way forever, it's just the start which requires lots of discipline and control.

Now, if you do decide to take the risk and join them, plan ahead! Make sure you let them know that you have embraced a new lifestyle and certain foods must be available for you. If they can't provide that for you, you bring your own food. Cook it, pack it and take it with you. In the beginning your environment won't take you seriously for two reasons: they don't know the new you, and secondly, you have given in to temptation too many times before. You will be encouraged to eat because they love you just the way you are, you poor thing. If they love you and truly know you, than they are familiar with the endless fight of making better choices. And you should get full support in your journey, not petty talks and pots of unhealthy foods. In traditional families refusing food might be a sign of disrespect. If you can't stand up for yourself and impose your will then don't attend the gathering at all.

It doesn't matter if your fears are weight loss related or not. The only way to overcome them is by controlled exposure and getting a whole new understanding over the matter. Don't hide in the house in the hope that one day your fear will disappear or diminish. Since fear is recorded by your subconscious defence mechanism, the only way to reduce or eliminate it is through exposure. Take one fear at a time and be proud of your progress. You are not in a race, it is just you putting the effort in to become better each day. Always stay focused on your goal and do everything in agreement with your heart and mind. You are your own boss, you make the rules by which you live! By being in control of your outings and parties, you will break many fears you previously developed.

Summary

You have to kill your fear! Find a strategy that works best for you and keep using it. With every fear you overcome you become stronger. A life lived in fear is not a life lived at all. Not being able to fully immerse yourself in life's beauty because you are petrified with fear is truly a shame. Wouldn't you rather live life at its fullest than wonder what if every minute of your existence?

Leave your safety bubble and explore! 90% of your horrible scenarios never become reality! Is it really worthy to neutralise it all for only 10% of what might happen. When you buy a lottery ticket the chances are less than one in millions, hundreds of millions to win. That has never stopped you from getting your weekly ticket, has it? The two things you lose when purchasing the ticket is money and a few minutes of your time. The possibility of winning is really low, but because the losses encountered are minor you take the risk of spending your money and time for less than a 1% chance to win. There is a slight chance, and yet you take a leap of faith. In life, your whole life, you have 10% chances of bad events, and you are petrified most of the time. You choose what is important to you in life. Becoming a millionaire overnight is worth the risk, whilst being alive and happy is not. Why? Because you don't truly believe in a life full of joy and achievement. Right now you are lost, and after so many times of trying and failing you are scared. You gave up on yourself and your ability to make smarter choices.

Fear is created by your own subconscious as a defence mechanism. Fear makes you pass on opportunities. Confront your fears by gradual exposure and start living a beautiful, full life!

Chapter 7

Leave your toxic environment

As I was getting better physically, emotionally and mentally I kept on asking myself this question: why did I fail so many times before?

It was becoming clear to me now how losing weight can indeed make my life better. So many opportunities suddenly appeared and I was having more courage to go for it. It wasn't the weight itself which made me stay away from the outside world, but the pain that I was living in. My inability to accept myself, to see my potential, made me say no to everything. I failed because I didn't truly believe I could do it. I failed because I didn't understand what was holding me back. I failed because I was hating myself.

Growing out of your pain requires a few skills. First, you must find the source of your pain. It could be anything really: bullies, family, a broken relationship, some traumatic event, a rubbish job, anything. Start sharing your frustration with the people you trust. Then observe your environment and notice how many people truly believe in your ability to change. The reason why you fail most of the time is because you don't have a real support group. You must learn how to become independent of your environment, because unfortunately it is very likely that your environment is holding you back.

Before finding my path I was part of a toxic environment. All my friends were drinking and partying, eating unhealthily and living a pretty much random life. None of them had real goals or any reasons to be better. And I became complacent in order to fit in that world. At home, as mentioned before, the eating habits were terrible and absolutely nobody I knew was doing any kind of exercise. With such a horrible environment and lacking a role model, how was I supposed to succeed in my attempts to lose weight and find my path?

Just like you I like to believe that I am an independent human being and I make my own choices. It might be hard to hear this, but you are the result of your environment. Take a deep breath and think of the similarities between you and your family and friends. Don't focus on weight issues or body similarities. Think of the lifestyle of each and everyone around you. Are any of them properly exercising? And I don't mean just occasionally when the sun is out. I'm talking here about a strict programme, about giving up outings and pizza for a better self. Are any of them trying to become happier and actively seek ways to improve? Are any of them working hard towards achieving greater goals? Most likely they are not. They are as complacent as you are.

For these reasons you must grow independent of your environment. You can still keep the relationship going and meet them occasionally, but preferably seek to spend more and more time with people who have similar goals as yours. I used to occasionally sign up for gym memberships and maybe drag a friend along as well. Due to the fact that my friend was joining solely to keep me company and be a good friend with no actual interest in embracing a healthy lifestyle, it didn't make much of a difference. We would grab beer and burgers after each workout, after all, we deserved a reward for our effort. And since I didn't know much about nutrition and fitness, it never crossed my mind that my body actually absorbs the food much faster after a workout and thus ended up gaining more weight. I never talked to any trainers at the gym or engaged in any kind of conversation with other members. Looking back now, I know I was not ready. Food was my 'best friend' in good and bad times and I wasn't ready for a healthy replacement.

Most overweight, fat, obese people, are compulsive eaters. And I was no exception. Food had been my addiction since early childhood. Food wouldn't scream at me, or make me fear, or beat me or punish me. It was people doing that to me. So why would I confide in someone? Food was my sanctuary of safety. And when you grow up with that conviction, it takes time to break the belief and make smarter choices. Getting over the abuse I had experienced at home, plus the unhealthy relationships I developed throughout my life took me a total of twenty-four years. And that is what truly happened. I can find a million excuses why I failed to change before, but the reality is that the pain was too much to handle. And I wasn't ready to let go of it. The healing process hurts tremendously. Bringing out all the dirt from deep inside you is a proper labour. You will heal and have the life you always dreamt of, but be ready to put sweat and tears into the process.

I am the kind of person who almost never dreams at night. When I was ready for change and I was growing out of my environment and pain I started to get nightmares quite often. Memories, fears, scenarios I thought of before, it was all surfacing now. Have you seen the saga *Twilight*? I was just like Bella. I was screaming and crying and punching in my sleep. I swear I would wake up exhausted. My brain wouldn't get any sleep and all those memories and fears were there day and night. If your pain is caused by the same people who are still part of your life, how can you truly heal? I know you must feel weak and vulnerable without your 'support group', but they are not actually there to help you get better. They hurt you in the first place and you must see them for who they are.

Acknowledging the influences the outside world has on you can be quite stressful. Using your reasoning you try to convince yourself that whatever you do is fully your choice. For example, that you willingly overeat or overindulge in alcohol, sex, or whatever form your addiction has. You firmly believe it is not an addiction or influence, it is your choice. Now call me crazy, but why would you willingly live a life where your weight makes you unhappy? Why would you willingly drink so much that your liver performs like it is thirty years older than your actual age? I doubt it is by choice.

I wasn't eating double portions by choice, although I was the one asking for them. I was overeating in the hope that my pain would disappear. It seemed easier to keep on eating than stop. And my environment despite a general well expressed concern over my weight kept on feeding me. Would the same people call for food delivery? Yes. Would the same people take me out for drinks? Yes. Would the same people bully me? Yes. You can see the behavioural pattern now and the reason why I had to free myself from that toxic environment.

As soon as my mindset shifted and I started to enjoy the benefits of losing weight I opened myself to the world. I suddenly found myself in the company of people with similar goals, people with more knowledge in fitness and nutrition, so I could actually learn a thing or two from them. Being part of a real support group gives you strength to cope with the daily struggles. The journey to healing is neither smooth nor challenge free. And when you are at your most vulnerable, that's when you need to be extra cautious and fully rely on your new environment. Being surrounded by people who understand your pain, your fear, your desire to be better, it is priceless. Having the right support group would ease your journey, because now you know that you are not the only one who has it hard in life. Although you don't like to admit it, knowing other people are struggling too makes you feel better about yourself, like you are not the only broken one out there.

My family always possessed the power to make me overeat. Abuse gives you the greatest power over anybody. My emotions are so intense when it comes to my family that my first instinct is to open the fridge and eat everything. Even to this day, my inner child believes that food will make things better. When I am getting criticism from my mum it wakes up so many memories and opens up so many wounds that all I can think of is food. And I don't mean salad and corn, but sweets and deep fried food. Food was my only comfort as a child and despite being a grown up now my inner child will forever try and resort to food. I'll tell you a secret that worked perfectly for me: stay away from the triggering factor. If there is a person, a place, a memory, an activity, anything that might make you overeat, reduce contact as much as possible. It is a skill that gets developed in time and it takes practice, but once you possess it your addiction will be under control.

Forcing myself into training has never worked well for me. My excuse: I don't like it, it's not for me, I get too sore. And my favourite and the most common one: I was not raised in a family of athletes. In fact I was only too scared to start because I had to learn everything from scratch. When you don't know stuff you can always learn. Acknowledging you don't actually know how to do it and seeking the right information to learn will bring you unexpected opportunities. I had to take tennis lessons in order to play decently. And the more I played the more I liked it. I played tennis with people who liked it and were putting the effort in, and I played with people too lazy to even return the ball. If I were to keep on playing with the wrong people I would probably have ended up hating tennis. But I said no to those whose game was not challenging enough and I decided to play with those better than me. I am a highly competitive person and I love to be challenged. I love to work harder and harder in order to achieve. By getting my ass kicked quite often, I had to put more effort in with every match. And with my extra weight coming off quickly, I would become more athletic and capable of finishing my matches.

My new environment helped me tremendously in sticking to the new routine and making tennis part of my healthy life. Getting my ass kicked was the best thing that happened to me that summer. When you are ready to become better you must surround yourself with the right people.

I wasn't sure if I was ready to go to the gym or not. I didn't know if I had the body confidence to go and sweat in a public space. What do you do when you are not sure? You go ahead and find out. To my surprise, for the first time in my life, being in a gym felt amazing. I felt as if I had finally given my body the respect and care it deserves. I had my induction with this trainer, a funny, fit guy. Normally, I would have felt intimidated and not talk much, just listen to the guy and wait for the awkward moments to finish. This time I was chatting relaxed, asking questions and wondering if he could help me improve my fitness knowledge since I had never really trained before. Accepting that I knew nothing gave me the courage to ask and learn. Before I knew it I was chatting to all trainers in the gym and asking for advice on pretty much anything. I had now become one of those girls that every overweight and shy person hates in a gym, a sociable, confident young woman who wasn't ashamed or afraid to explore the world around her.

I think it is really important to mention here that I was far from my desired body weight. I was still chubby and fluffy but I didn't care anymore because my new environment was not bullying me for being overweight, and it was encouraging me to become better and achieve greater things every day. A different mindset, a different attitude towards life, took me amongst people who were actually appreciating me, who saw value in me. And getting appreciation for your efforts is uplifting. It is a validation that what you are doing now is right for you.

Not everybody in my old environment accepted my change and slowly they drifted out of my life. I didn't have to put any effort into that. In my new approach to life, gym, healthy eating and at least eight hours of sleep per night were a priority. And many of my friends or family never got that. They still don't. I would normally go to the gym in the morning and spend at least two hours there. Sometimes more. It wasn't all about training, but chatting, changing, having a drink, it all takes time. And I would get calls to go for coffee and have breakfast at 10–11 am. My friend, I have been up since 6 am. It's lunch time for me as soon as I am out of the gym. My answer was 'no thank you' 95% of the time. And this friend actually said once, 'it's all about the gym with you now. I don't get to see you at all'. And I thought that instead of embracing my new lifestyle and maybe joining me for a session since she had missed me that much, she phones me to judge me for my choice? With such friends who needs enemies anymore, right?

Partying and drinking was again a big part of my old life. And since the country where I come from lacked a proper law enforcement and the patrons love money, going clubbing at a really young age was not a problem. By the time I was sixteen I could easily enter all clubs. Before you get excited, things have changed now and the enforcement is a little bit more serious. Life was easy back then. I wasn't swimming in money, but I had a decent allowance which allowed me to enjoy myself reasonably. As I grew older I kept the habit and it even got worse as I reached university. I used to think that all that drinking and partying made me feel fulfilled. Gave me purpose. Sort of a reason to live until the next party happens. Every time I would start a new diet I would suffer so much that I couldn't drink or party anymore.

It wasn't the addiction of food or alcohol that would necessarily make me doubt change, but the fear of not fitting into my environment anymore. Without the drinking and eating fast food at random times of the night, who was I? Well, as I later came to realise, I am actually quite an impressive woman full of energy and able to achieve. But back then I was scared to rise above a life I was familiar with. And that familiarity brought me nothing good but pain and emotional misery for over two decades.

Getting out of your comfort zone feels really difficult and challenging. Putting yourself in a position where you are judged by your family and friends feels scary, too much to handle. But the reality is that good shit only happens outside of your comfort zone. As I always say, you are already a mess, how bad can it be out there? Just because it has been tough on you lately or for too many years now, it doesn't mean you can't do better.

Let's take a toxic relationship for example. Almost every woman has had one at some point. That's how you learn and grow, no regrets. How can you know you have found a good man unless you are able to compare? My toxic relationship was long and painful. We both knew we weren't good for each other, but we were equally scared to let go. In my case we kept switching the victim and abuser positions, so it's only fair to say that we both had the same responsibility in the failure of the relationship. Back then I was convinced a relationship involves pain, misery, fighting, depression and binge eating. I can tell you that I was wrong. Of course there is no perfect relationship and life is full of ups and downs, but when the core values and feelings are lost such as respect, compassion, understanding, support and it is all replaced by guilt, failure, sadness, regress and negative emotions in general, you are better off. It is freaking hard to let go and acknowledge your reality, but you do want to get better, don't you? In the last year of my toxic relationship things went south rapidly. My sex life was nonexistent, couple fun activities were nonexistent, we were fighting all the time, both gained excessive weight and we were both overdrinking. And the cherry on the cake was depression. We both had it but neither of us knew that. We were too young and inexperienced to spot it and address it.

We lived like this for a year. Why? Not because of love, but because of fear. We had been together for so long we were scared to face the outside world individually, separately. We were one fucked up entity. There was love and respect when we became a couple. And lived beautiful moments together. And the support we gave each other in the hardest moments of our lives will forever stay with us. Unfortunately, we failed the time test, and a few years later we were racing towards the end of it all. I could not have taken that relationship any further. I gave everything and I was now drained. I had to let go.

After we broke up, in full consent from both parties that we can't be a couple anymore, I often had panic attacks. And I would eat so much. Because the wound was fresh I felt like a lost puppy. I didn't know which way to go or what to do. To explore the outside world or to lock myself in the house? To party like never before or just eat lots of junk and cry? It was a feeling of relief mixed with fear.

Remember how good things happen outside the comfort zone? It took me two years to get over everything, to fully heal. In this time I lost all the extra weight, ninety freaking pounds. I regained my confidence and defeated depression. I started living again. I was training five times a week at least, I was doing yoga and meditation, I was taking care of myself again. I would do my hair and nails and wax and own my womanhood. I felt like the freaking phoenix bird. My sweet, sweet rebirth.

I could have never found myself again whilst being in that relationship. You see, things might be good before they turn nasty, and that's normal, but keep an eye open to spot when shit goes south. Don't be scared to escape pain because real love doesn't hurt. It can be stingy at times and perhaps you want to stab him with a fork or pen, but you would still feel love whilst doing that.

Although your partner might play an important role in your current state, don't underestimate the influence others have on you. Any sort of connection which doesn't fit in with your new lifestyle must be cut. If not, you risk returning to the same old mess. Once you make the call to change you will get resistance from your environment. They will either tell you don't change you are great just the way you are, or criticise the way you do things. Or the time you invest in the new, better self. Don't resent them because they do not understand your new mindset yet. Instead of feeling down now is the time to squeeze out the poison. Let go of those who bring you down.

Don't be scared you will end up alone. Your new life will bring lots of people your way. And it will be the right ones who will help you grow and support you in making the best choices. When you exercise and eat right and sleep right and find yourself as a woman again, you will become confident and strong. You will choose who to have around you. You won't be surrounded by random people who don't bring value to your life anymore.

It was 2012 and I was enjoying my Spanish class in uni. I wasn't putting much effort into other modules, but Spanish was by far my favourite – I used to watch lots of Spanish series as I was growing up so the language was associated with fond memories. I had even bought myself a text book and all. In front of me were seated two girls who I'd never spoken to before. One of them was tall and fit like a model with beautiful gold hair down her back. The other one had such a beautiful face and dark long hair and her perfume was so strong. I had always thought they were out of my league and I had never spoken to them before, until this day. The teacher made us sit together and surprisingly they were super nice too. I didn't know then the role these two young ladies, Andra and Liana, would play in my transformation journey. Without their love and support I could never have done it. From that day onwards they became my new best friends. Remember how the good shit happens out of your comfort zone? Having a drink with Liana later that week was the beginning of an amazing, unforgettable journey.

Often your change will start years before you consciously take positive action. It can start with a new job, new relationship, new friends, only later in life you will find out the true purpose of your new circumstances. When I met Andra and Liana I had no intention of losing weight or taking care of myself again. I had just ended a long, painful relationship and I was completely lost. I felt empty and I feared a lot, I feared a new life, where I could make my own choices. Being in a relationship for the last six years, I was definitely not looking for anything serious again. I wanted to be alive again, do stuff, explore, get my ass of the sofa and meet new people. As I got to spend more and more time with these two ladies, it only took a few weeks to feel as if I had known them for a lifetime.

Andra was more sensitive and she was all in for a healthy lifestyle. She is such a good woman with morals and values and committed to her relationships. Liana back then... she was more like me. She had recently regained her freedom after a long relationship, she didn't care much about training and healthy eating, she wanted to explore and enjoy her freedom. For the next year Liana was my partner in crime in absolutely everything. Damn it, we wanted to feel alive and we DID! I remember Andra telling us to slow down, to care for our bodies more, to sleep more and party less. But we did not stop. After being in such long relationships, Liana and I needed something else. Maybe we were right, maybe we were wrong, it didn't matter. We lived every second of every moment. I remember sitting at dinner drinking and making stupid jokes and thinking why do they accept me? Why do they like me? They are so beautiful and smart and educated, so posh compared to me. What do I have to offer them?

My girls have a huge heart. They took in a wounded, lost girl and gave me strength to cope with life. I felt loved and cared for. I had nothing to give them in return and I will forever owe them the world, because with them I discovered unconditional friendship and love. I swear I was as broken as one can be, and it was the first time in my life when I was giving less and receiving more from my environment. Liana and Andra started my transformation by showing me that outside my toxic world there is love and care and compassion and true friendship. And every time I had to face hard times I would retreat into my safety sanctuary, Cluj town. That's where my girls were, my true support. Liana and Andra, thank you, I love you and I will forever owe you!

As I kept on saying throughout this chapter, you are never truly alone. If you open yourself to new experiences you will meet the right people to help you progress in your journey. And because you are so broken right now, you will be confused as to why somebody is helping you, but remember that good shit happens outside your comfort zone and toxic environment. Just because you have been unfortunate enough to have only bullies around you, it doesn't mean love and friendship don't exist. You just have to go out there and find it!

Summary

Leave your toxic environment! If the same people who have hurt and bullied you are still around when you start your transformation journey, how can you possibly succeed? You need a truly supportive environment, full of people who have the same goal as you.

Your change is to be praised and not be taken as a joke. If you don't stand up for yourself and let your environment know that you are serious about change and your life is not a joke, nobody will. When people around you don't speak the truth to your face they think that's soft love. When people around you refuse to accept your pain and need for change, they are failing you. Being stuck in a toxic environment is extremely dangerous and you are the only one who can battle your way out.

On your transformation journey you will come across wonderful people who will add tremendous value to your life and build memories and friendships which will last forever. There is no stronger feeling than having a common goal and facing similar challenges alongside somebody else. Overcoming those challenges together and always offering and being offered support is truly empowering.

And always remember: GOOD SHIT HAPPENS OUTSIDE YOUR COMFORT ZONE!

Chapter 8

Learn and grow

I am about to share with you something nobody told me as I grew up. You must always have role models and mentors! As you progress in life it is normal to find new role models and mentors constantly. In order to grow and learn, you have to become obsessed with successful people. With people who faced the same struggles as you who can now teach you how to overcome all the mess based on their experience. There are many reasons why I didn't have role models, as you will soon discover.

In my country computers and the internet were only entering the market in the late 1990s. If you could afford a computer and broadband you were a superstar. All your friends would come over and play games and watch movies. Access to information therefore was not as easy or broad like today. The main source of information came from TV. That meant that if you missed the show because you were in school or outside playing, well that was it. The replay was normally in the morning when you were in school again. Your only hope were your friends. Perhaps somebody could tell you what happened.

You can see how difficult it was to have role models or do proper research into something. Or have access to the latest developments or studies. I got to say we were pretty dumb compared to kids these days. The internet made it possible to hear and see things when they're actually happening. LIVE! And it can be accessed time and time again and shared and downloaded and it's all happening so fast. I didn't have all that as I was growing up. Perhaps I could have made better choices if I had access to more information. I was still playing ball at sixteen years old. Good old times.

My parents bought our first computer, mine and my brothers', in 2001. We suddenly became the cool kids. The house was next to the university campus and the students had free broadband. So we connected a cable to their router and had free internet for years. It took me a while to learn how to use the computer. It was mostly used for games and movies though. Now that I think of it, none of us was doing anything productive with it.

I always complained I was fat and I didn't know what to try anymore, but I never took the time to learn more about nutrition or training. Nobody is born almighty. It's up to you to be open to new experiences and learn. And funny enough, the more you read the more passionate you become about a particular topic. But I wasn't reading shit about it. I wouldn't buy a book or open an internet page to research weight loss. I would only listen to stupid people who didn't know a thing about losing weight. Stuff they heard before and were 'kind' enough to share. Most of what I tried was based on hearsay. How could I have been this naive and stupid you might ask. Well, when there is nobody to guide you but the hate for your body and life you will always go for self-destructive options. Because involuntarily, you seek to punish yourself for the misery you feel and live every day.

I know I am using strong words and some of you might be shocked. That's because you never took the time to analyse why you are doing certain things. I can find 1,000 excuses why I didn't do it right, but deep down I know there is actually only one reason why I did it: I chose to punish myself!

Life is a choice. Your actions are a choice. What you eat is a choice. What you wear is a choice. You choose to stay alive! So from now, before listing 10,000,000 excuses why you did or didn't do something, remember it was a choice. One of my favourite books is *Feel the Fear and do it Anyway* by Susan Jeffers. She says there that there is no right or wrong choice, only different ways. That's freaking brilliant. If you hold on to the pain of a 'wrong choice' and don't seek to understand why you made that particular choice, you will live with guilt for a very long time. And guilt only brings more guilt. And in the end you are left with the incapacity to forgive yourself and acknowledge that in those given circumstances you chose as wisely as you could.

I look back and I know why it took me twenty-two years to change. I know there wouldn't have been any other way because I had to learn my lessons. I had to overcome my emotional mess before making better, smarter choices. When there is no love how can you protect yourself from yourself?

I can blame it on my parents – which I did for twenty-two years – on my environment – alcoholic friends, lack of knowledge, lack of role models, external influences, life difficulties, fucked up relationships, abusive father, death of my dog, fear, weather, festive seasons, anxiety, the list is endless. In reality it all comes down to me making a choice to employ excuses instead of finding that one reason that would have helped me heal. All because I was not ready for change.

There are many ways to lose weight, too many to write it here. And yet obesity is going up and there are more depressed mums out there than ever before. Why?

I was never able to accept my body. And as the years passed and the jokes and abuse I received from people around me increased, so did the hate towards myself. You see, in the beginning you hate your body. You know you don't actually fit anywhere because people stare at you if you eat in a public space, and you can't join your friends for certain fun activities due to the extra weight, and back then I was the only fat kid in my classroom. So I knew my body was the problem. Later in life, as more and more abuse was directed towards me, I started resenting life itself.

So my initial problem, being overweight, now became a bigger issue. Emotionally I was a mess. When the subject of jokes is always the same – your weight – you become resentful towards your body. I learnt to hate my body. My toxic environment made me hate my body. As a baby you know only love and positive emotions. You don't believe me? Have a look at the little ones laughing at a flower, smiling when the breeze gently blows in their face, laugh hysterically when opening and closing the wardrobe door 1,000 times. They are pure and full of happiness and love. Unfortunately, as you grow up and your environment expands and you get in contact with more people and have many experiences, you lose touch with these positive feelings. A toxic environment, school, church, family, friends, neighbourhood, all that contributes to you hating your body and life. By all means it is not your fault. It's not about weakness, it's about being repeatedly reminded how unworthy you are. No matter how much you fight it, eventually you will believe it yourself. And the feeling of worthlessness will become, in your head, one of your core flaws. So wrong!

And yet true. The power of the masses has long been recognised over history. When the majority of people around you 'jokingly' abuse you and you are not shown any respect, love, value or appreciation, you will grow to believe you are not worthy of any of these. It is a true labour to open your eyes and remove the toxic people from your life. Because it could be your own family or the dearest of your friends. I had to let go of my past and see my family for who they really are. They abused me because it was easier to do that than fix themselves. They are all overweight to obese. My father is the abuser. My mum is the victim. My brothers are the result of a divorce and broken father-son relationship. My grandma is a self-absorbed, money driven old lady with barely any love or consideration for us. And also she was Mum's first abuser. Uncles, aunties and cousins have rubbish marriages and professionally are far from successful. With such a mess in their own lives it comes as no surprise that their pain became mine through constant abuse.

I love the access to information these days. Any time you are in doubt quickly get the phone out and in a matter of seconds you will find your answer. It is truly amazing, you are like a walking fuckin* encyclopedia. And yet you don't have the answers, do you? One of the rules by which I live is this one: don't ask the question if you don't want to know the answer. The reason why you are still fat, unhappy and depressed in 2018 is because you are not asking the right question. You are scared to identify the core of your pain and answer the damn question. And by not asking the question 'where is my true pain'? you cannot outgrow the emotional misery you are in right now. My rule can be self-destructive when that one answer stands in between you and greatness. Ask the right question and find the honest answer.

If the true problem was your weight you would join a gym, do some classes, eat some healthy shit and in no time you will look amazing. But that is not what you are doing, is it? You go for diets which could permanently damage your health, you eat and force yourself to vomit, you go on starvation mode for a few weeks before your big event, you take pills and shakes, you do stupid shit that will never, ever work.

Oh, and you never move your ass off the sofa because you don't know which kind of exercise is best to lose weight. Any exercise that will get you off that sofa,   I guarantee you it will work. You know what you do is fucked up and takes you nowhere, so why are you still doing it?

I will answer for you. Because you are an EMOTIONAL MESS! Because every new diet you try is another attempt to punish yourself for the pain you live in. Unless you acknowledge that change must be internal and external, chances are you will continue to be stuck. First step in your transformation journey is waking up. Observe your environment and see it in its true colours.

- Is it the right environment for you to succeed in your transformation journey?
- Does it understand your current pain?
- Does it understand why change is needed?
- Are the people around you willing to support you?
- Are they able to push you into achieving your goal?

If the answer to any of these questions is no, get away from them now! If you are twenty stone and as miserable as any human could be and your best friend tells you how amazing you look and nothing about you has changed, then she is not your friend. Or likely she is fat too and wants you to stay the same so she doesn't feel bad about herself. I told you opening your eyes is true labour!

When I see two to three generations together and they are all obese I feel sorry for them. Especially the youngest generation. I used to say that obesity runs in my family. That genetically I was born fat and I can't change that. I was stupid, OK? What I should have said is that the eating habits in my family are shit and they are all medically unhealthy and obese because they can't stop eating stupidly. Instead of using their rubbish eating habits as a reason to do better, I used it as an excuse to become complacent and gain more weight by the day. You see how it is up to you if you want to become better or not? I chose to live like them. I was not ready to stand up for myself, acknowledge the toxicity of my environment, and rise above their mess. I became complacent in their mess and I made it my main excuse to stay obese.

Kids are and always will be the result of their family. If they become felons the parents are responsible. If they are alcoholics, the parents are responsible. If they are fucked up or a success the parents are responsible. Parents are the role models and the main influence in a kid's life. What happens in real life is this: if the kid is a success the parents assume the credit for it; if the kid is fucked up it is someone else's responsibility. Parents, it doesn't work like that. When applying the chain of causation from childhood to adulthood you will be found responsible for the upbringing of your kids.

If as a kid you are obese and unhappy and do stupid shit to self-punish yourself for your inner pain, the parents are at fault. Unless the kid has health problems, which is a completely different story, you are responsible for his habits. Who taught him overeating? Who taught him to eat crisps and chocolate bars for lunch? Who taught him to drink coke instead of water? Who told him to stay still and watch TV every evening because you are too lazy to take him to the park and play?

When I tell my mum these things she says she tried her best. And I know she did. In between being a victim and a businesswoman, she would try her best as a mum. It was her lack of knowledge, it was her inability to escape abuse, it was the shitty society she was brought up in that prevented her from living to her full potential and thus be a brilliant mum and woman. I love my mum the most and she will always be my role model, but I choose to raise my son differently. Based on access to information I choose to put my best into my son's upbringing. He will forever be my reason, my drive and never my excuse.

After you have observed your environment in its true colours remove the poison. Any person who is not supportive of your change, any person who makes you feel guilty for wanting to do better, anybody who makes the journey harder for you, limit your contact with them. Or let go completely. Once you have assumed your reality and publicly announced you are ready for change, there is no need for pity or soft love anymore. From that moment onwards you need to stay focused and you need to be pushed in the right direction by the right people. Explain to them how you expect when invited to a barbecue party to find healthy food and plain water on the table. And if they ignore your request or tell you that a one-off is OK, they are not good for you anymore. A true friend will forever respect your choice and remind you how fuckinging great you are. A true friend will believe in your ability to achieve.

The past doesn't matter anymore. The new you made it clear to them that change is in place and they had better comply. When I started losing weight, my environment was exciting for a while. 'Finally Stef will lose the extra weight and reveal her true potential. People will soon discover how amazing she is'. My 'true' friends have always considered that my obesity prevented people from acknowledging me or my awesomeness. Anyway, so the journey started. I was extremely disciplined with my eating. For a few good months there were no exceptions at all. One of the rules I imposed on myself foodwise was this: food is just fuel, don't overcomplicate it. After a while I would get comments like, 'do you eat anything other than salad, lean meat and controlled portions of carbs'? Suddenly, the support turned into criticism. I was eating too clean now. Do you believe this is sustainable? they used to ask me. You will get fat when you start eating again, they would say.

Your environment will need time to accept your change. The best time of your life yet requires new dynamics in all your relationships and only time will decide if they are strong enough to last or not. You stay focused on your goal and build the discipline. Don't listen to people anymore, because that's what you did all your life and here you are now. No good comes from soft love and lying.

Summary

The unlimited information you have access to these days must be put to good use. Don't use it just as a means to communicate or get online recognition, but use it for a greater purpose – to improve your life.

Learn about nutrition and training, learn about meditation, experience new stuff, because that's the only way to grow. Technology has made everything accessible so there is no excuse.

If your environment brings you down or keeps you stranded at the same level, let go of it. Believe in yourself and make it clear to everybody that the new you will not take any BS.

Chapter 9

And I got pregnant

Change is not easy, but once you overcome all your fears and make a definite decision to reach your goal, all your actions will take you there. The universe will align to support you in your journey to greatness. After years of struggle and pain I was finally living at my full potential when I found out I was pregnant.

I had mixed feelings about it. After the excitement settled, I realised I was going to get fat again. I never considered my body was going to nurture a baby, and all the weight I would gain had a higher purpose. Throughout pregnancy I regressed a lot. My main fear initially was gaining the weight back. What I didn't know then was that gaining weight would bring back all the pain. On top of the pregnancy hormones I was overwhelmed by the past. Memories, insecurities, doubts, all the emotional baggage would soon return.

Not long after I started having nightmares almost every night. My subconscious quickly woke up my worst fears and I was once again on a journey to pain and desperation. One hour I would be excited about my growing bump and listen to his little heartbeat, and the next moment I would be full of insecurities and stare at my small size clothes. Having to get my tiny clothes out of the wardrobe and make space for the bigger sizes was so freaking overwhelming. Every time I replaced clothes in the wardrobe I cried. I have a red lace, backless dress. I dreamt of wearing a dress like that my whole life. When I got it I was so happy and I would wear it with so much pride and confidence. It felt as if my feminine side was peaking, I felt empowered and in control of my life. I remember taking it out to box it and I turned around and faced the mirror. I put the dress on top of my tummy and it wouldn't even cover a quarter of my front. I started crying instantly. In my head all was lost. There was no freaking way I could ever fit in that again, not without ripping it apart at least. I boxed it eventually and tried to convince myself that I would regain my body in the near future. I said to myself as soon as I give birth I can return to my great looks. I was so naive. My body would never be the same again.

The thing with pregnancy is that very few mums speak the truth. You have mothers saying it can be challenging sometimes, but that's only partially true. I found pregnancy extremely challenging, and not just physically, but emotionally and psychologically. The pregnancy hormones were making me proper crazy and I cried most of the nine months, but it was more than that. I have always been super active and determined to achieve great things. My energy embarrasses people around me. I remember when I was doing my master's degree and all 99% of those young women wanted was to get married and make babies. All I ever wanted was a big family and to be a stay-at-home mum, they used to say, and in my head I was wondering why are you studying and wasting time and money on your education then? I have always been different. My goal was money and recognition. Work, work, work. It never crossed my mind to settle and have a family. That's for weak women, for those who can't escape the stupid stigma of society. After finishing my studies I was applying for graduate jobs and I was pushing every day towards getting my dream job and finally making my degrees worth something.

I didn't know that life had a completely different plan laid out for me. I got a temporary job at a bank and that's when I met the love of my life. It was my friend's wedding on the 2nd of May back in my home country. We had been friends for almost a decade. I had to go and be with her on the big night. I had plane tickets booked and all. I was ready to party. And then, one morning, I get a call out of the blue. A nice lady tells me she'd found my resume online and there's a job and if I wanted to pop in and have a chat. A job at a bank, I thought, I have to take this. I went there all nervous thinking it would be an interview, or at least some kind of cat fight for the vacancy. It turned out it was only me and the job was mine under one condition. No days off or travelling for the first sixty days while at the job. With a broken heart I called my friend and told her I have got to take this job and thus I won't be making it for the wedding. According to my friend shit happens, get the job and move on.

So I went ahead and took the job. My first day at the office was on the 16th of April 2015. A glorious day I will forever remember. There he was, the most handsome man I have ever seen. With a perfect smile and kind eyes, the future father of my child closed the door in my nose and didn't allow me to enter the building. It all had to do with the company's safety regulations I found out later on. The rest is history. It was love at first sight for me, it took him a few months to feel the love, but we got there eventually.

That was strike one from life. Finding love. We soon moved in and it all seemed a fairy tale. Being with him was my antidote for every wrong in my existence. Three months later, strike two from life. We decided to open a powerlifting gym. All our law and finance degrees were soon covered in dust, forgotten in a box. And so did our dreams of becoming the perfect employees. Entrepreneurship here we come! Three months down the line... strike three from life. I am pregnant. If that's not moving fast and skipping steps in a relationship, then I don't know what is. It takes a couple of years to make these kinds of decisions, and with us it was all happening at lightning speed. What the fuck do we do now?

Be stubborn and stick to your plans. The gym plans went ahead and soon got real shape, the baby was growing nicely, and I was becoming crazier by the day. Everything I never wanted was happening. Everything I ever wanted was too far away from me... so far that I let it go. I couldn't get over my own thoughts. You are a typical woman who finishes her studies, gets pregnant and becomes useless. I didn't have much respect for mums back then, honest confession. I was tired, I felt sick, I was pregnant and fat, I had baby brains and my hormones transformed my lovely personality into a monster. I was living on the edge. Throughout my pregnancy I felt disabled. I was restricted from living my life normally, I couldn't even wear proper shoes. I had days when I was so tired I couldn't even go to work. Most of the time it felt that anything I put near my mouth would make me sick.

My inability to work more, to be more productive, frustrated me. That was all I wanted and pregnancy was restricting me from achieving my dream. Since I couldn't keep up with my job and opening the gym, I went on maternity leave in order to finish up the gym and get the dice rolling. I would stay at the property from 7 am to
10 pm. By now I was seven months pregnant and had gained at least four stone. It was a massive effort to keep up with everything. I had to deal with deliveries, watch the workers, go buy stuff all the time to speed up the work, fire people for not working fast enough. It was complete madness. Despite the tiredness and the fake contractions (thought I'd give birth there), I felt fulfilled for a little while. It was my desire to achieve, to be productive and my hard work was now paying off. Soon after opening the gym I had to slow down. I was trying to push myself too hard but my mind and body wouldn't keep up. In my head now I was completely useless.

I wasn't training anymore either. I stopped at six months and a half. My tummy was so big it become unsafe to lift. So far you can see how pregnancy prevented me from living to my full potential. And that's the thing nobody tells you about pregnancy. You cannot be yourself, you can't do the things you used to and you can't stop crying or peeing yourself either.

Pregnancy is extremely challenging on a woman. Until the maternal instinct develops it all feels like a sacrifice. Some women get the feeling early, others, like me, don't experience it until after birth, which means that pregnancy poses a great challenge. Morning sickness is another big fat lie. I was sick twenty-four hours a day, seven days a week. I would especially be sick when I was tired, which in the first term of pregnancy is most of the time. I kept on training as usual in the first term, trying to keep my fitness up, but most sessions would end up with me puking behind the gym or in the closest bin. And I was so sore, like never before. I could tell my body was consuming extra energy and it was trying hard to accommodate my baby.

There were brighter days though. When his little feet would poke me and wake me up in the morning. When I would sing to him and he would dance inside me. And seeing his cute 3D face on the screen was heart melting. I knew he was perfect. As a soon to be mum, despite the pregnancy struggles, you know what you have got is too precious. I could feel his craziness and playful spirit even then. It was his hobby to poke his daddy at night and wake him up.

I am not saying that carrying a baby is impossible or it's all bad news, but the truth is that you don't know what to expect from it. There are too many variables and each body responds differently to the pregnancy changes. Personally it was hard to accept my incapacity as I never thought I would be a mum. With that in mind you move on towards other goals.

When I was twenty-three years old I was diagnosed with polycystic ovary syndrome and was told that if I want to become a mum I need to undergo surgery and the sooner the better. At that point in my life I had never thought of that. And the news didn't make me angry or upset either. Quite the opposite. I was glad I wouldn't have to cope with a surprise pregnancy. I left it there and I never took any treatment or underwent any surgery. A few years later, after losing the extra weight and living a balanced life, my body regulated itself and my fertility increased. Of course I didn't know that and surprise! Baby is on his way. It was a miracle, a shock, happiness and lots of wonders. I know what I am good at and I own my life. I love being in control of my life and my environment. I didn't know shit about pregnancy or motherhood. How do I know if I am ready? What if I can't care for this baby? Am I going to be a bad mum? What defines a good mum? The list of questions was endless. My own thoughts were driving me mad. I doubted myself and my ability to raise a happy kid. I was expecting the worst. And I was already feeling guilty for ruining his life in the future.

I have this belief that babies choose their parents. I believe in a higher power energy sort of thing that gives you challenges so you learn. Life's an endless journey of learnings and I wanted to stay faithful to my beliefs, so I kept on looking at my tummy and asked my son 'why did you choose us? What do I have to learn from you?' And I trusted that my questions would find the answers in the near future. You see, when the present doesn't seem to make any sense, and you slowly lose hope, you must believe there is a higher purpose. Give it time to reveal itself to you, give yourself time to exist and understand. We all have different beliefs and they were created as a result of our experiences or knowledge accumulated over time. Unfortunately, experience sometimes can be a disability and prevent you from growing and accepting new ways.

Due to the fact that I grew up with an abusive father, I never thought I could be a good parent. I mean, if nobody showed me how to do it right then how can I learn the best parenting skills? The fear of ruining my child's life was so strong that I made the choice to never have one. I would rather deprive myself of motherhood than do a shitty job. I do believe at birth we are pure and good and full of love. And throughout life, instead of enhancing these feelings and spreading love and positivity, the environment turns all this into hate, greed, egocentrism, competition and many others. And I didn't want to carry such a burden on my shoulders. I didn't want to be responsible for bringing up another soul into this world full of wrong already. My experience turned into my disability and my decision to say no to motherhood was, at that point, very reasonable and supported by evidence and facts. Only after I became a parent I understood. As my mum used to say 'wait until you become a parent and you will understand'.

If this baby hadn't chosen us and I had to choose him I wouldn't be a mum now. It was my conviction that motherhood is not for me and I would actually be doing the baby a favour by not abusing his little soul later in life. Baby boy, thank you for choosing us. You are my highest achievement and having you has been my greatest journey towards improvement. You make me a better person every day. I promise to love you forever and your happiness will always be my priority.

Even if you don't have negative convictions like mine when it comes to parenting, let me tell you one thing: you are never ready to be a parent. Even if you think you are, trust me, you have no idea what is coming your way. It is pure madness wrapped in love. This chapter is not meant to push you away from becoming a parent, quite the opposite. It is meant to tell you the truth about how challenging pregnancy and parenting is, but more importantly to make it clear to you that you are responsible for the upbringing of your progeniture.

You know how most first-time mums are terrified of labour? I was so big and uncomfortable I couldn't wait to give birth. In the week before the estimated due date I would tell my son how badly I needed him to hurry into the outside world several times a day. Ready or not you are coming anyway so you might as well hurry, was my very first motherly thought. At 3 am on the due date my waters broke. Did you know that only 5% of babies come on their estimated due date? I always knew my baby was special. Everything that night happened like in the movies. My waters broke and it was literally squirting out of me... lots of it. What happened next is beyond ridiculous. Trying to wake up my partner to go hospital proved to be challenging and hilarious. 'Babes, my waters have broke, your son is coming. His reply: 'Stop joking around, go watch TV if you can't sleep'. 'Babes, I am serious. Look, the bed is wet.' 'Stef, seriously, I am tired, I won't play your game'. And that is when I realised I had played lots of pranks on him that week. Something like: 'shit, I have contractions, my waters have broke, babes. He is dropping.' You know, normal jokes you make to your super stressed partner waiting for his first son to arrive at any moment.

When he was finally up I decided to shower first. I couldn't have gone to the hospital to give birth covered in womb liquid. It's a matter of principle – you must always be clean before going to the hospital. Even if there is a real chance you will shit yourself within the next few hours. As I was showering my contractions started. I am like OK, not bad. I can manage this, my pain tolerance is high today. Victory, I thought! You gotta keep it positive in those moments you know. Panic never helped anybody and it is extremely easy to slide into fear and terror during labour. And by not accepting the pain, it hurts even more because your body will try to stop something which cannot be stopped – the delivery.

Anyway, we finally got in the car, but not before I packed myself some food. I despise hospital food and I knew I would be hungry very soon. I was always hungry. My partner is a very careful driver and never disturbs anybody in traffic. He always takes his time, but not that night. He suddenly became a Formula 1 driver on the empty streets of Birmingham. Of course we didn't know where the hospital was and had to set up the satnav first. And the way there was so confusing, with funny corners and one-way streets and my contractions were happening every three minutes already. It was all happening so fast I couldn't have been happier. During one of my contractions my babe said the most beautiful thing: 'Boo, I swear my body feels your contractions'. He was living that moment at the same intensity as me. I knew that very moment that he will be there for me throughout the whole labour and delivery.

Weeks before the due date I kept on asking him if he is interested in joining me in the delivery room. His answer: I don't think so. He wasn't sure he had the emotional strength to watch the childbirth. I quote: 'Babes, what if it is so traumatising that I will never desire sex with you again'? Somehow his question made perfect freaking sense. I love him enough to respect his choice and I wasn't keen either way. I had prepared myself for this moment for nine months. You know how sometimes you are sure things will happen a certain way but actually you have no real facts to believe that except your guts? For months I kept saying I will give birth in the squat position. My Oli thought I was crazy and kept telling me to stop squatting around the house, it is too dangerous to do it that way. We kept on laughing and all, but deep down I knew my body would be the strongest in that position.

As we finally arrived at the hospital we didn't know the way to the delivery wing. So we got out of the car with the suitcase and all and ran to A&E. In there we were told to go around the corner until we find the wing. We ran back to the car, two more contractions, and started driving around the hospital yard. We finally found it and we made our way in.

First thing: put on the horrible clothes I had packed weeks before. That night gown was horrible indeed but it was the only thing that would fit me. Seriously, I was massive. I got checked and was told I would be kept there under supervision since my dilatation had started already. I could feel my baby was in a hurry to join us and spare me the prolonged labour hours.

I got moved to a room a few floors up. I guess they were trying to save light since I was the only one there, because they didn't bother to switch on the lights in the hallway. Anyway, there I was in a room with Oli wondering what would happening next. The contractions were every two minutes now and shit was getting serious. I kept walking around and standing all this time. The minute I would lay down I would puke. The pain was unbearable in that position. The contractions made me tired so I decided to sit on a fitness ball. I thought it must be there for a reason. I have to admit that it was comfortable sitting on it, so comfortable I would have dozed off in between contractions. I had only three hours of sleep before labour started and I was drained. And I was so hungry, but I was advised not to eat before delivery. The occasional puking was not helping either.

The pain was starting to increase and I could feel my boy dropping. I called the midwife and I was told I would get checked at 8 am, which meant roughly two hours later. I insisted in a very bossy tone to get that hand inside me and check me out. In those moments you don't have time to be polite and smile too much. After minutes of arguments she finally did it. And guess what? Oh dear, your dilatation is about seven centimetres. You are almost ready. My face was definitely expressing something nasty.

Eventually I got moved to the lower floor again and put in a room with the nice comfortable ball in. I wanted to live the moment fully so I didn't accept any medicine or epidural. It was all raw and organic. I had to prove to myself I was strong enough to do it without medication. It was my first test as a mum and I wasn't going to fail it. Also, I didn't want a csection because recovery is longer and more painful. And finally, I wanted to return to training asap and a surgery would have definitely delayed the process. All the reasons in the world to go through the pain of labour, don't you think? Honestly, I don't regret my choice and I think it actually completed and closed the circle of pregnancy. In a metaphorical way it ended the inner pain pregnancy had awoken, the nasty memories of the past which haunted me throughout those months.

If you develop the ability to accept the physical pain of the labour, this is the supreme test of motherhood and womanhood. If you manage to get that baby out, one way or another, what else can stop you in life? But mums quickly forget what they have been through and the pain and mental challenge you had to overcome. It all becomes a memory and you don't give yourself the credit you deserve for what you have achieved. Just because it is 'normal' doesn't mean it is freaking easy.

I am not going to give you details of what happened in the delivery room, but I will share this. The fact that my partner was there throughout and witnessed the pain and joy of birth made our relationship the strongest it has ever been. I earned his highest respect, and despite his fears it wasn't an event which left him with post-traumatic stress disorder.

His love made the whole moment beautiful and his support in those moments was all that I needed. Many times you let the fear grow based on scenarios you create. Or stories you have heard. But life has ways of showing you that you are many times stronger than you think. Your ability to cope in the hardest times will even surprise you.

Summary

The fact that you carried your baby for nine months and then got him into this world is priceless. Your sacrifice must not be forgotten or overlooked. You earned the right to express yourself and claim the respect you deserve.

Despite the hardship of pregnancy you love that baby the most. And in those times when you doubt your choice or ability to make the right decisions, remember that motherhood is too complex to be understood or lived in a few days or hours. You will discover new things about yourself in this journey and you will get stronger every day.

Allow yourself to feel the pain and the joy. It is not a smooth process and it is never the same for any two women. Your story is yours. Live it!

Chapter 10

Post-natal depression

Generally speaking, all focus is on the childbirth. Once the mum and baby are feeling well and get discharged everybody assumes it is all under control. As a first-time mum you are going crazy inside that beautiful head of yours. What do I do with this baby? I mean, I have no clue. Is it like in movies when the maternal instinct wakes up and I suddenly know how to care for my son?

It took a while for my maternal instinct to wake up. I was definitely unprepared and I tried to use the knowledge I gained by watching my nephew for a few hours in the past. Aunty duties are nothing like mum duties. On the way home from the hospital the weather was extremely hot so naturally we opened the car windows. After enjoying the first breeze, I panicked. What if the breeze is too strong or too cold for the baby? I asked Oli to roll up the windows, but we couldn't breathe in there. So he kept on opening and closing it the whole way because I couldn't decide what was best for the baby. Finally we arrived home and that's when the fun started. First night it was OK. Junior slept in his crib and woke up only twice. No massive screaming or anything too extreme, we were pretty happy with it.

I was thinking how I had got the grip of motherhood already and was going to cruise through. Yes, admittedly I was wrong. The second night the screaming started. Hours of hysterical crying, with dozens of failed attempts to calm him down. Breastfeeding was going OKish, changing nappies was not the problem and the room temperature was OK. What is the problem, son? I never got an answer to that. However, I did spend most of my nights on the staircase walking up and down the stairs. It was the only thing that would calm him down. As days passed the crying overnight became unbearable. Oli was helping as much as he could and he had his fair share of walking around the house.

During daytime he would still have plenty of crying episodes. I have never seen a baby crying this much. He would only sleep on my chest and every attempt to put him down would wake him up. I tried using the chest wrap but of course he rejected it. He wanted to be in my arms, on my chest, all the time. Any accessories I tried to use to ease my life he clearly rejected. As such, I was covered in puke and bowel most of the time. I had no time for myself at all. My breasts were leaking milk like crazy. I was neglecting the house. I was neglecting my partner. I was exhausted. I socially isolated myself because of all the reasons mentioned above and before I knew it I quickly dived into a nasty post-natal depression.

And I couldn't accept what this baby did to my relationship. How it changed the dynamics and now I wasn't getting any more attention. As a couple we couldn't do fun stuff together or even spend an hour in peace. It was all about attending Junior, day and night. Life as I knew it was completely gone and I was resentful with a passion towards the mum life. With the gym freshly opened Oli was working mad hours, sixteen hours per day. I was by myself with the little one most of the time. However, on weekends Oli would finish early and we would sit down and catch up. Not anymore. Junior was extremely jealous and he wouldn't even let me sit next to Oli. The minute I would get closer he would scream his lungs out. Wow! There was an inner fight, or many I might say. I wanted to make Junior happy, I wanted to spend time with Oli, and I needed to care for myself as well.

The start of the mum life proved very tough for me. Surprisingly, Oli adapted very well and quickly and had unlimited patience with him. He used to tell me it will get better, it is a transition period for all of us.

I remember him praising me for what a good mum I was and how much I cared for our son. And how I was able to sacrifice myself for his sake. Newborns require lots of sacrifice from the mums. Maybe you do it because you have to, maybe out of love, regardless, all your attention is on the baby. It's not a choice, but a must. I know I was a mess and I had no idea how to most of the time, but Oli believed in me and he knew I was doing my best in the given circumstances.

And my body… I couldn't believe what pregnancy did to me. I was deeply affected by my appearance and I had doubts I'd ever lose the baby weight. I kept repeating to myself that I had just had a baby and it is normal to be out of shape. It's normal to be overweight and weak. I did not manage to convince myself of that at all. The opposite. The more I'd say it the more it would hurt. Weeks after having Junior I decided I needed to come back as a woman. I had to take control over my life again and accept the new dynamics. I had to work out an action plan to own motherhood and womanhood.

For a good while I didn't know I was suffering depression. I assumed that's what mum life was all about. Sadness, exhaustion, isolation, crying, mostly negative emotions. It was Oli who triggered the alarm. I love this man more than life itself and I am the luckiest to have him. Without him perhaps I would never have recovered. It was the middle of the night and Junior was crying like mad. He kept on going for hours. I lost it. I gave him to Oli and I started punching the wardrobe, the doors, the walls. I don't want to imagine how Oli perceived me but he said this: 'Where is the woman I fell in love with'? I took a break from punching the walls and I turned around. And he told me how I have become someone else, how I am always bitter, unhappy, crying, refusing to leave the house, unable to accept Junior and the new dynamics. How I complain all the time and yet I am not doing anything to improve my life. It was the hardest conversation I ever had and yet the most needed one. He saved me from a life of misery and unhappiness. By speaking the truth to me, his truth, he opened my eyes. It wasn't Junior, or my body, or my lack of sleep, or the new dynamics which made me feel that way, it was depression. It was an identity stronger than me which took control of me. And until I acknowledged it, I couldn't take positive action to recover.

That morning I woke up and wrote down all my feelings. It was so painful to have it all written down. Black on white, that's who I was at that point. All my emotions were negative: sadness, guilt, failure, social isolation, inability to focus, desire to stop existing, anger, frustration, lack of appetite, insomnia. I cried so much that day that I ran out of tears. It was the most painful realisation and awakening I have ever experienced. I felt responsible for my current condition and I blamed myself for failing to clock it. I sought help straight away. I started therapy and I was diagnosed with severe post-natal depression. It took me months to defeat it, but the pain was so strong I will always remember it.

Every morning I didn't want to wake up. I hated opening my eyes in the morning... why am I still breathing? I used to ask. I just wanted the pain to stop. It was suffocating me. I had no love for my baby. I never thought of hurting him, but I couldn't bond with him at all. I used to look at him and blame him for my pain. In my head he was the only one at fault for my misery. Junior's crying was annoying me and I wasn't feeling that maternal instinct to care for him and attend to his needs. Most of the time I would sit on the sofa in the living room and stare at the wall for long periods of time. I would hold Junior on my chest and sit there feeling nothing.

I was exhausted and hungry but I couldn't sleep or eat. Junior was crying that much I gave up on sleeping at night. I'd just sit at the edge of the bed and cry and wonder when it would all stop. Only my partner and my therapist knew of my condition. Like most mums out there, I would fake it in the outside world. I would pretend I have it all under control and I'm living the dream. In my head I had to be the perfect mum, wife and housekeeper. I had to act like everything is normal.

I was scared of being judged and considered weak. A failure. It felt that all eyes were on me and they were just waiting for me to crack. And maybe some were doing that indeed, but looking back I know that all that matters is myself and my family. Depression doesn't allow you to voice out your pain because that would reduce its power over you. You want to speak and share but the words are not coming out, because the same depression keeps bringing back thoughts of worthlessness as if you don't deserve a better life. And when your head is full of your own negative thoughts how can you take positive action to recover?

I felt alone. I felt as if I were the only mum struggling in this world. I tried to chat with some friends who'd had babies roughly the same time as me. I was giving hints that I was overwhelmed and struggling. All I would get in return was how much they love their babies and how becoming a mum completed their lives. Now they have a reason to exist and they were all so happy in their bubble. It made me feel like shit. Either they were faking it or they had adapted to the new life without a struggle. Regardless, I felt alone. I had Oli as my main support but what I needed to hear was that I was not the only woman finding it hard. That there were other mums who suffered from depression and recovered. I needed to know that I could get better, that I can love my baby and accept my new family.

Throughout all this madness which lasted over six months, my Oli has been amazing. His patience and understanding for my condition meant the world. I would share with him my darkest thoughts or feelings and he would give me love in return. He would tell me how I look better, how I smile more, how I am slowly coming back. And how my love for our son was obviously growing. Slowly but surely. Being validated for every little effort I did by the person I love the most was a great impetus for my recovery.

When depression is in control you lack the ability to focus or have any drive to do anything at all. For that reason many mums never identify or recover from it. Firstly they don't know they are suffering with depression, and secondly they are waiting for motivation to make a change. Unfortunately, depression will never give you a break and you must find ways around it. You must own your life and consciously take positive steps to a better self. I had the luck to have the greatest communication with my partner and when times were hard none of us shut down, but we discussed and tried to find a solution. We refused to give up on our relationship.

Based on Oli's feedback I was able to identify my depression. It wasn't motherhood or my son who was making be bitter and sad, I was suffering a real mental disorder and I had to seek help immediately. If you are a new mum too, or soon to be, pay attention to the changes you might encounter. Of course with the baby's arrival things will change, but it doesn't have to be negative. Until the new routine settles and you get a hand on mummy duties you will most likely be tired and look like a zombie. However, if you still have the strength to smile and your baby is your world then don't worry, you are doing great. If, however, you look at that baby and wonder why you did this to yourself and regret that your life can never be the same, keep an eye open for possible depression.

Always ask for feedback from your environment. The truth can be harsh sometimes, but unless you ask nobody will approach you to ask about your wellbeing or mention any negative observations related to your latest behaviour. Everyone is scared of mums, especially crazy mums! Being a mum is not horrible and is definitely not the worst thing that happened to you. It feels like that when depression settles in, but once the pain is gone all that's left is love and peace.

The recurring negative thoughts you experience during depression are horrible. You feel unworthy of life, alone, undervalued, and you feel life as you knew it has ended and all that's left is unhappiness, exhaustion, frustration and there is no way out of it. You generalise every event and don't consider the given circumstances. When my son was four months old I took him for a short visit to a friend's house. It was his first visit I believe. Because of my anxiety I would keep him away from people or public spaces as much as possible to avoid him catching a virus or something. My friend, Anna, forgot to mention she already had a few guests over and the house was a bit crowded. As I got there my son got scared and he was agitated throughout the whole visit. I had to stand up and walk him around the whole time. Half of the time I was locked in a room breastfeeding. And what made it worse was that Oli was not there. I never thought then that Junior was feeling my emotions. I was panicking and my anxiety spiked. It was Junior's first visit and Oli was not there. What if I needed him? I was a complete mess. And my boy picked up on that immediately. Of course my depression would not let me see things this way, but he was more scared than me. He was in an unknown environment, full of people, with an emotionally shaky mum. I called Oli to come and pick us up and take us home. I was exhausted and angry. My first visit since birth and it was an utter mess. I quickly jumped to generalising and promised I'd never leave the house again. Junior was impossible and I hated being out with him. I felt my life was horrible and I had no idea how to make it better. For weeks after this event I locked myself in the house. I would even do my grocery shopping online. The depression made me jump to this conclusion: you can never enjoy yourself with Junior and there is no hope for the future either. The depression cumulated with anxiety intensified all my thoughts and feelings and that evening, unfortunately, the negative attitude won. Just because your situation is hard now it won't be like that forever. Think and acknowledge the circumstances of every unpleasant event, try and be the baby. If I were Junior, and I have never been around ten people at once in a room, would a party make me anxious? Of course. Even an adult would feel intimidated. If Mummy is an emotional mess and fails to give a feeling of security and calm to the baby, how can the little one be composed?

When I decided to get better I realised how little control I had left over myself. It was so bad that I couldn't feel the motivation to do anything. My mind decided to make a change, but it was as if my body was disconnected from my brain and refused to respond to any command. That's when I understood something truly important: motivation is emotion based. And when you are not well emotionally, and if you wait for motivation to be your saviour, you might never recover. It was a precious lesson because from that day onwards I stopped waiting for my motivation. I made myself an action plan and the only thing that kept me going was discipline. I had to get better for my family as I was not willing to lose the love of my life and fuck up Junior's life because of a stupid depression.

Discipline is what helped me recover. I used to make a weekly activity plan and stick to it no matter what. Myself and my recovery became a priority and most of my efforts were going towards that. I would accomplish all my activities and tick them off before going to sleep, and although a degree of flexibility regarding the execution was required it would get done eventually by the end of the day. The activities were meant to bring focus back on me and break the negative thoughts. I would, for example, meditate, train, stretch, take a shower, put make-up on. I had to shift the attention back on myself as a woman.

I started training again four weeks after birth. I'm not encouraging anyone to do so, but I went ahead with it without medical clearance. Seeing my body in such a state was too sad, and I knew that despite the brutality of pregnancy and delivery, it was strong and ready for the losing baby weight challenge. I started with body weight workouts at home and they felt like the hardest workouts of my life. I was battered. My back was hurting, my pelvic area was a mess, my joints felt like jelly, my abs were non-existent and my flabby arms hadn't preserved any strength. That was the perfect cocktail for disaster. Honestly, I didn't think of giving up on my training at all. The pain during training was bearable compared to the thought of giving up on myself again. I promised myself ages ago that I will never become complacent again in anything in life, and I am a woman of my word.

The first three weeks after birth were really tough. We couldn't have intercourse, but despite my depression and the zombie mode I still desired Oli a lot. The connection we have during sex is amazing and I genuinely thought it would help me relax considering my struggles as a new mum. Three weeks later it happened and it was not what I expected at all. And not because I had recently delivered, but because of the baby himself. Remember how I told you my son was super jealous? I was convinced he had superpowers. Due to Oli's conviction that intercourse must not happen in the same room with the baby, we moved into the other room. The mood was settled and the excitement was there, when Junior suddenly woke up crying. Of course I attended to him and after ten minutes he returned to sleep. I went back into the room ready to try again. A few minutes later Junior woke up again. I am not sure if this has ever happened to you, but second interference is definitely a mood killer. So my long-awaited passionate physical contact was far from my expectations.

It became clear that Junior would cry every time Oli had his hands on me. Hence the thought that he had superpowers and could feel when Daddy was touching Mummy. I wasn't aware then that breastfeeding creates a crazy bond with the baby, and indeed he could feel all my emotions including arousal. Junior's constant reaction made my sex drive fall dramatically. Depression reduced my desire for intercourse too. I've always been a highly sexed person so I knew the benefits of sex on myself and my relationship. In my previous relationship the sex became non-existent for the last year so I was familiar with the frustration and lack of confidence which results from a poor sex life with your partner. I knew that unless I bounced back to normal my relationship would be damaged permanently. Knowing Oli he would have had the patience for me to return to 100%, but he would have never forgiven me for being weak and giving up on myself.

A woman's body is brutally abused for nine months during pregnancy and delivery, then you have to learn how to bond and care for a little screaming creature and it is just so much to cope with overall. The changes are extreme and you are stepping into a completely new life. If on top of that you suffer depression it feels like that's it. Fuck motherhood. Fuck womanhood. Fuck life.

You are completely entitled to feel this way. But let me tell you something. That child who you can't bond with right now will soon become your life. Your partner who you resent a lot for being the man and not having to go through all this will be your rock and give you the support that you need. However, you must acknowledge your reality and be willing to put effort into getting better.

A strategy which worked brilliantly for me was planning ahead. You expect certain stuff to happen naturally, and if it doesn't you quickly blame it on your partner. And worse, you create crazy scenarios in your head and push it all to the extreme. If your sex drive is gone due to depression and you shut down completely don't be surprised if your partner is not showing any interest either. Or perhaps after a few failed attempts he has given up. As humans we perceive emotions and body language and act based on the message we are getting. If your body is a no access area he will pick up on that and act accordingly. What I did to prevent causing more damage to my relationship is schedule intercourse. Literally! I know it sounds weird, and the desire to do it should come within and be spontaneous and all, but when you know that your depression will never let you feel that emotion again you take steps.

You create your own circumstances appropriate for sex. I synchronised our calendars and sex was booked in at least twice a week. I would make sure it was booked in late in the evening when we were both home, and no matter how long it would take to settle Junior or how tired we were we would not go to bed without it happening. Like anything good in life, you must put effort into it. I am talking about your relationship. If things are not right destiny will not solve your problems. If you both shut down and don't put effort into fixing whatever is wrong you will eventually either have a fuckeded up marriage or split. Don't take his love for granted. As humans there is only so much we can take. If you are depressed, overweight and unable to take control over your life and take positive steps to get better, he will eventually get fed up. And trust me, he is not to be blamed. As a post-natal depression survivor, I can honestly admit I was a proper pain in the ass.

When you two met you were full of life, love and joy. You were positive and able to control your life. You were outgoing and fun. Sex was aplenty and spontaneous. You would wear sexy outfits and own your womanhood. Ideally you were confident and ready to take on challenges. Taking care of yourself as a woman was at the top of the list: hair, nails, waxing and make-up was a must. And now… well, it is a different story. As a new mum the baby takes all your time. You are mostly covered in puke, sweat and bowel. Your sexy outfit has been replaced by saggy clothes, probably his. And what is the point in showering if you will stink again in no time? On top of that not so appealing appearance, your hormones are a mess. You cry and complain all day long, you're lacking sleep and it's been ages since you had a nice hot meal. That is not to say you cannot come back even stronger. But you must put effort into finding your inner woman again. Imagine if your partner had undergone all these sudden changes, would you still be attracted to him? Unlikely. You would however be willing to offer support throughout the recovery process. Having a baby comes with a price that your body and mind must pay. And that is understandable. But if you choose to stay this way after getting a grip on motherhood too, well, don't expect a massive improvement on your relationship. The man's duty is to be there for you and help you come back. If you choose to stay depressed, overweight, weak, unhappy, frustrated and take no action whatsoever to be the woman you used to be, don't be surprised if your relationship will go south at lightning speed.

If adapting to the new mum life proves to be a struggle, ask for help. I know you want to be a supermum and have full control from the beginning, but it is not possible. The change is massive and you must give yourself time to accept the transition period. And that thing you see on TV, the moment you see the baby and the love shoots through the roof, it is not necessarily a lie but there are plenty of mums who don't feel like that. I didn't. He was a stranger who turned our lives upside down. It took months for my love to grow. What I can assure you is that the more you love the baby the more you will accept and enjoy motherhood. And one day, before you know it, the pain will be gone and all that's left is endless love. All the pain you feel now and all the darkness will disappear and make space for an empowered mum, ready to take on anything.

Summary

Post-natal depression is real and requires active steps to be taken in order to heal. Don't suffer by yourself, share your pain and seek support. The reaction you get will amaze you for sure. It is the depression forcing you to believe that you are being watched and judged as a mum all the time. It is the depression convincing you that you are alone in this journey and you must stay this way. Whenever you struggle, ask for help. Your close friends and relatives will gladly help you out and support you.

Constantly ask for feedback from your environment. If you feel you are not yourself and the sadness is unbearable and the struggle gets overwhelming, you must ask for feedback. One symptom of the depression is the inability to identify it. It has its own identity and it will take you over without you realising it. As a new mum you will need some time to adapt and things will be messy for a while. That's normal. However, if you dislike your baby you cry constantly feeling sorry for your life and the recurring negative thoughts are with you most of the time, so trigger the alarm.

Start by speaking about it with someone close to you, someone who makes you feel safe and has lots of love for you. Even if the other person might be shocked or not able to advise as much, she or he can help you seek specialised help and make sure you and the baby are safe. Speak out, speak out, speak out!

Once the depression has been diagnosed you have got to pull yourself together and take steps to recover. Remind yourself every day why you must get better and what is at stake if you fail to progress in your recovery. Be disciplined, be aware, make time for yourself. Don't try and be a supermum from the beginning, it takes time to settle in a routine that works for you and the baby. Forgive your partner if he doesn't know how to cope or he's scared. Be open about your feelings as that is the only way to keep communication open and save your marriage. You both have to work things out and be there for each other.

Always remember that the baby will soon be your whole world! You must protect that at all costs and try your best to make the best decisions in the given circumstances.

Chapter 11

Truths about motherhood

As long as you live, you learn. As long as you learn, you grow. You grow to become better, wiser, stronger. Those times when your whole world collapses, it's only a phase in your existence. It's a lesson to be learnt and used wisely in the future. Overcoming today will make you greater tomorrow! Most mums must be like phhheww! I know it sounds like a cliché, yet only by taking one day at a time will you own motherhood.

Let's start by agreeing on something: motherhood is freaking hard. Being a mum is by far the hardest task, job, challenge, anything I have ever had to do in my life. As you grow up you are faced with many challenges and lots of stressful situations. I remember my student days when writing a 1,500 word essay was a giant task. I would spend days worrying about my deadline, never writing anything down or even opening a book. Instead I would go out and drink because the stress was overwhelming. Whatever stress you are dealing with, most times it can be postponed or managed. Most of the time it is not even real stress you're dealing with. It can be avoided with better time management. Motherhood on the other hand happens every second of your life. It's happening as you are reading this.

I'm sure you must have seen one of those funny movies with new parents trying to cope with a newborn. The reality is much worse and it is almost never funny. Being depressed with a newborn is far from funny. Having no family or friends to help you out is surely not funny. Being covered in puke, breast milk and bowel is definitely not funny. Acknowledging there is nothing left of the woman you used to be cannot possibly constitute a joke. And finally watching your relationship go south quickly is not the comedy of the year.

Current times don't allow you to be a stay-at-home mum. With rising costs of living and ridiculously expensive child care, paying the bills and providing enough is a challenge for many families. As such, most mums are working too. There is also an increase in the number of single mums who are the sole provider for their children. You get the point: as mums we do everything, raise, educate and keep the cheeky monkeys alive. We manage a house, cook, clean and shop. The modern mum has one or two jobs. She also runs errands and has dozens of bookings throughout the day. And that's the modern mum, a freaking superhero keeping everything in order.

You can't do everything at once or in the same day. As a new mom I used to live under constant pressure that I had to do everything perfectly. From caring for my baby to managing the house and the business, losing weight, regaining my sanity and confidence, taking care of myself, having a social life and being the perfect supermom.

Yeah, that's kind of not possible in the beginning of motherhood. You know yourself as being strong and active and capable, but now you are a mum. And for a very long time the baby will be your only priority. And even if you do manage to squeeze in certain activities, it will be completely different now. Don't let it frustrate you too much. Think about the other millions of mums who experience exactly the same adaptation issues as you. You are not alone and you are definitely not weak!

I genuinely thought I would return to my old self a week after birth at the latest. I would clean and cook and take care of my house, baby and man and spend a few hours per day managing the business. And have hobbies again. One week after birth I was still seated on the sofa wondering what I was doing. How am I going to cope with all this? And I would look around the room at the diapers, the tissues, the mess. It was crazy. I couldn't even remember when I had last had a shower or a hot meal.

It was so frustrating to accept that I couldn't do it all. Or at least not as well as I used to before I became a mum. I know now that my house won't be clean again until my son leaves for university. My advice to you is to prioritise. Everything in life is as important as you want it to be. You are the one making the final calls on your life. Make a list of your priorities and stick to them.

I only iron the necessary stuff now. And sometimes I don't even fold my laundry. I realised it was a massive waste of my time. Junior loves to drag them all out from the wardrobe and dive into the pile of clothes like it is a freaking pool. I used to hoover two or three times a day after each his of meals. Now I just pick the big pieces with a tissue and hoover every two or three days. He can't stay still when eating, he loves running around and spilling it everywhere. I disagree that what he does is misbehaving. He is a young soul exploring his surroundings. I love his curiosity and courage. Some people, including my own mum, say the house is a mess. Do I really care? My goal is to raise my son to be a good man and father, not an obsessive cleaner. Motherhood is not about satisfying the outside world but making yourself and your family happy. I know for sure that you bury yourself in house chores for the sake of what people might think. You feel like you are in competition with every other mum out there. You have to change that. Firstly, it is not a competition. All mums are doing their best. What matters to you might be of no importance to another mum. Secondly, your time as a mum is too precious to waste on random, useless chores. I am not saying to live in dirt or walk around in stinky clothes, but there is a fine line between what is necessary and compulsive cleaning behaviour.

I chose to give up on doing unnecessary activities and decided to take that time to focus on myself. I am now in full control of my life! Being able to nurture myself as a woman ultimately makes me a better mum and wife. Most of our parents couldn't escape society's rules and influence and raised us completely different than how we raise our kids. As long as I can remember, my mum has been a business owner. As I grew up she was always busy and tired. The little time mum would get to be at home was all about cleaning and cooking. I wanted to spend quality time with her, not just be by myself in the room playing computer games. But I never voiced it out and she was too busy and absorbed in daily chores to acknowledge that. You always assume your kids would love to spend time with everybody else but you. That's what you think as the parent, but the kids actually love to do fun activities with the people they love the most in this world. As you grow up you don't remember all the cooking and the cleaning. You reminisce about the beautiful memories you have with your loved ones. And sometimes there are not enough memories. Probably because of my past, I want to be here for my boy. Not metaphorically but to literally be part of his life. I want to play with him as much as possible, do fun stuff together, nap together, make sure that in the future he will remember my love and not my compulsive cleaning. My priority is to make my boy smile and keep him happy at all times.

My mother never took time for herself, she had three kids and a business to run. She gave everything to her environment and never took care of herself as a woman. And as I grew up I witnessed a beautiful, strong woman losing her inner power. High levels of stress and tiredness quickly turned into illness. As the days went by under this hectic life and mad schedule, I witnessed wrinkles appearing on her face at a very early age. The bad eating habits made her overweight. And the daily self-sacrifices made her feel drained and unhappy. She sacrificed herself for us. But I wonder if that really is the way.

As I grew up it was hurting me to see her like this. Every day was another fight for her, but she would never slow down and take a step back. I owe my mum everything and without her I would not be at this stage in my life. I appreciate everything she did for me and my brothers. However, I want to live a different kind of life. I want to offer the best to my environment and be able to make them happy and meet their needs, but at the same time I matter too. Trust me when I tell you that neglecting yourself as a woman and not taking good care of all your needs does not make you a better mum or a better role model. I learnt from mum's mistakes. Her pain became mine. A mother with anxiety and depression becomes an emotional burden to her children. Eventually your kids will pick up on your misery and feel responsible for it. Because lack of time is the main excuse you use as a mum, your family will start feeling guilty for putting so much pressure on you. Stop being a victim and become the mum. Be in control! You are the one setting up the schedule in the house, so how about prioritising?

Taking time for yourself is the best way to start your transformation. You will discover that you are so wired you have forgotten how to relax, and you have completely lost the ability to not give a crap. If you are stressed and anxious and drained, you are not a positive influence in the house. Your selflessness is the main reason for your inner pain. You give too much and there is nothing left for the woman inside you. And that is one of the main mistakes mums make. How come? I am a mum, I don't have time for myself. Bullshit! You choose to neglect yourself and you choose to live in pain! Motherhood is about raising and educating the kids. Make sure they turn out to be decent adults and good parents. Motherhood is not about endless house chores, out of this planet cooking and immaculate clothes. Motherhood is not a contest. There is no jury evaluating your performance. And even if there was, you choose what matters in life and assume it.

As a mum you live under two constant pressures: your inner one and the outside one. I am seriously angry at the society we live in. Let me explain. Why is it OK to wear sweatpants as a mum to go to the supermarket, whilst if you wear nice clothes and heels you are getting judged? Why are obese mums defended whilst the fit ones are being judged? I don't mean to offend anybody but society has got it completely wrong. It belittles all mums. What society actually says is that once you become a mum you don't actually matter as a woman anymore. More than that, it actually labels you if you desire to escape the mum etiquette and reconnect with your inner woman. You go to train in a gym instead of cleaning the mess in the house, wow, you are a selfish mum.

You choose to sit down and listen to a bit of relaxation music instead of cooking for hours, wow, you are mistreating the kids. There is plenty of BS coming from the outside world.

You know why they are doing that? Because you allow them to. If you were to voice out what matters to you and what your priorities are, I guarantee you none would dare say anything. Your confidence would shut them down. Even more, there are high chances of getting their respect and admiration. There is nothing more powerful than a mum in full control of her life and environment. If someone announces the intention to visit I clearly explain that my house is a mess and the little spare time I have for the next few days are dedicated to myself and my son, so I'll call back when I am ready to have guests. They think I am crazy! Perhaps I am. But unless I prioritise and stand my ground my environment will take over. Nobody truly cares what's best for you but you.

You don't have to pretend everything is perfect. You don't have to pretend you are never exhausted or overwhelmed or fed up with endless chores. It is OK to speak up and let your environment know that this momma has had enough and it is time to take care of yourself again.

I know you are probably scared of being judged, of being called a weak mum, incapable of endless sacrifice, being called selfish and self-absorbed. How dare you take time for yourself. What have you done to deserve it?

Motherhood is freaking tough. The toughest. And you must voice it out. Speaking the truth will release the inner pressure you experience every day. That pressure forcing you to smile and pretend you live a perfect life. You will be surprised but let me tell you a short story. I am an extremely honest person and I always voice out my thoughts. Since I have become a mum I defeated post-natal depression, have lost six stone, launched two businesses, saved my relationship, wrote a book, been through many challenges and yet never have I cared about anyone's opinion. You are a mum, you have to slow down and stay focused on the baby. Now that you are a mum your place is not in the gym anymore. As a mum you are only allowed to go to the supermarket in your house clothes.

The kind of shit people have told me shocked me. The funny part is that nobody asked me how I felt, what I wanted to do, and how I wanted to approach motherhood. They had already decided for me. I, on the other hand, decided to show them that I am a different type of mum. In the beginning my environment was shocked that I didn't respect the norm imposed by society. Later on I became a role model for the same mums. I showed them a different path – my path. A way of motherhood where I am empowered and happy and healthy and I sleep well and I eat well and I have amazing sex, even better than before.

Accepting and voicing out the challenges of motherhood empowered me and helped me escape the stupid norm imposed by society and helped me live life to the full. I respect all mums because I'm one myself and I know how hard it is. However, I feel sorry for those ones who pretend their life is perfect. As my partner always says, if young ladies hear me talk about pregnancy and motherhood they might never have babies. I am honest and I love sharing my truth. Unfortunately, people don't want to hear the truth, they are too scared to accept their reality. I am a mum and it is an amazing journey. I learn new things about myself every day. At the same time it is bloody hard and sometimes I feel like throwing in the towel. But motherhood happens every second of my life and all I can do is manage and cope.

I choose to take care of myself and do less ironing. I play for hours with my boy and we eat sandwiches. I often don't have time to cook complicated recipes. I teach him dancing and we start our day by playing tunes in the house. What? Instead of planning and hurrying and running like crazy to get it all done? That's my way of parenting. It is not perfect and it doesn't happen without being judged by the outside world. I completely assume my choice to raise my son to be happy and confident, to be kind and persistent, to be a great husband and father. Ultimately you decide how you want to live your life. What kind of mum you want to be. What kind of wife you want to be. What kind of woman you want to be. Whatever your call is, make sure it is your choice and you don't react to outside pressure.

Summary

Being a mum is the hardest job ever. And you are doing an amazing job. You are covering all their needs. Now is the time to rise and shine, mamma.

Start by prioritising. You can't do everything in one go, you might have superpowers but you have still got only two arms and legs. Think deeply what really matters to you and rearrange your priority list.

Learn how to be selfish again. Unleash your inner woman and make yourself happy. Making time for yourself doesn't make you a bad mum. Quite the opposite. If you are rested, happy, fulfilled, if all your needs have been attended, you are ready to give to your environment more than ever before.

There is no such thing as perfect parenting. There is no parenting school to learn more either. You decide how you want to raise your cheeky ones and the kind of investment you are willing to put into their upbringing.

Chapter 12

Fitness and motherhood

Motherhood has made me reevaluate everything about my life. Who I am and what I stand for. Stuff that seemed major before means nothing now. I have learnt what is really important in life and what true drive is. Everything good in my life now happens because of my son. Junior is my reason to be better every day.

Being pregnant and seeing my weight go up by the day was terrifying. I used all kinds of lotions to improve the flexibility of my skin. I was desperate to preserve my body in a decent condition. And to my surprise, every pregnant woman I have known in this life was equally worried about the changes her body suffered during pregnancy. I have not heard one mum saying 'oh, I am so happy I gained five stones in pregnancy and my lower tummy is covered in huge stretch marks'. Every pregnant woman complains of discomfort, joint pain, back pain, getting out of breath, being tired, the list is pretty long.

And then when the baby comes you suddenly put all this behind you. Well, you shouldn't. Unless you take positive steps to improve your body it won't get in amazing shape by itself.

And I don't mean getting a six-pack, I mean getting your strength back, your pain free body, your ability to run your day and not feel drained most of the time. Just because you gave birth your body will not automatically bounce back into shape. You might lose the baby weight in a decent amount of time, but how are you going to cope with the weakness of the muscle and joints?

During pregnancy our body stores more fat which is necessary for the development of the baby. What happens post-partum is that you are left fat and weak. In pounds you might weigh the same, but in inches and shape there will be massive differences.

Of course the post-partum body will suffer permanent changes. Once you decide to carry a baby you automatically sacrifice your body. Personally I was left obese with wider hips, stretch marks, loose skin on my tummy, saggy boobs, saggy ass, bleeding gums, a black tooth, and probably many others of which I didn't even care anymore. Psychologically I was depressed and emotionally I was not very well either, crying every five minutes for months after giving birth. What I am trying to say is that the immediate period after birth is crucial. Obviously you want to bond with the baby and deep down hope your baby will be different and not keep you up all night. And that's when reality slaps you in the face. For a few weeks after you had your first baby some time is required to accommodate to the new life, to the endless needs of a non-stop crying baby. But once you fall into a routine and it gets easier it's time to focus on yourself a little bit too.

Believe me when I say that it is up to you to make motherhood easier and more enjoyable. And the only way to do that is to nurture your body. You can't undo the stretch marks, or the wider hips, or bring your breasts back up naturally, but you can lose the baby weight and get your strength back. Sitting on the sofa and complaining that being a mum is exhausting and is literally draining you will not improve your situation. It seems easier to cry about it and wait for life to turn things around, but unfortunately that's not how life works. You have to put your shit together and get the work done. How is fitness going to help with motherhood? Let's list the benefits of losing the baby weight: no more being out of breath, becoming more agile, improved movement, keeping up with the kid, gaining confidence and feeling sexy. Then the benefits of exercising correctly: getting your strength back, building muscle, improving resistance and stamina, energy boost, releasing endorphins and managing your anger. Your whole life will change drastically. You will feel at your best and indeed be unstoppable.

The weaker your body is the harder it is to adapt to the new life and do your best. If you are in pain most of the time and your energy level is minimal how can you not be frustrated and angry? Nobody can easily accept such massive negative changes. Every new mum compares her previous self with who she has become now. And unless your adaptation is as smooth as possible, you might feel resentful towards the new dynamics.

After birth I was left at 200 pounds (I'm five feet so picture that). My breasts were exploding with milk and leaking most of the time. My pelvic area was a complete mess with terrible pains and discomfort. My joints felt like jelly. My whole body was at its weakest, with pain and aches all over. And then it was the actual aesthetic of my body, that image in the mirror that was hurting so much. I couldn't believe what was left of my body. I honestly didn't expect pregnancy to damage my me so badly. My energy level was extremely low and every activity felt so draining, like I had to force myself to accomplish anything. After birth, ironically, I was feeling weaker by the day. Keeping up with my baby's needs plus trying to manage the house and care for my partner proved too much for my weak body. As the days passed and there was literally no improvement, I decided to take control of the matter.

It was time to return to exercising. Wow! I was super excited and all that was left now was to find time for myself. With my baby being extremely clingy and unsettled I had to improvise. The only thing that would keep him quiet was my partner driving him around. So whilst I was exercising, Oli would drive around and watch our son. This arrangement worked perfectly for all of us. I didn't use my clingy son as an excuse not to train, but I found a solution to my problem. Important note here, sometimes you need help. Don't feel guilty or ashamed to ask your partner or the family to watch the kids whilst you train. It might feel uncomfortable in the beginning, but once you notice the benefits you will soon enjoy your break from parenting.

I'll never forget my first post-natal workout. I was doing body weight exercises which before pregnancy was easy work for me. I thought I was going to die like ten times throughout the session. I felt my body breaking in a million pieces. Internally of course. It was freaking hard. I puked in my mouth quite a few times. Never has exercising felt this hard. Did I want to quit? Funny enough no. The physical pain was tough to cope with, but the happiness, the fulfillment, the emotional release I felt throughout the session made it all worthwhile.

My form and technique was so off. My squat looked more like a good morning and my lunge was only halfway through, but it didn't matter. I was putting 150% into those workouts and that's what made a difference. Emotionally and psychologically, I felt an instant release. I could feel frustration, anger, tiredness, all sorts of negative feelings leaving my body. In those thirty minutes I wasn't a mum anymore, I was a woman. The focus was shifted back on me and my needs. And when you give everything to your environment, a little attention for yourself feels like heaven. It will instantly recharge your batteries and get you ready for a new round of motherhood. Exercising after having a baby is not just physically challenging but emotionally and physiologically too. You might feel selfish for taking time for yourself. You might feel guilty for not doing house chores instead. You might feel judged by others. And then the endless fight with your inner thoughts: 'I don't have enough time', 'I am tired', 'I'll lose the weight in time', 'I'm not ready', 'My body is too weak', 'I look OK like this', 'I am a mum', 'I don't care what I look like', the list is endless.

The main reason why you exercise as a new mum is to be able to care for your baby without being resentful. As harsh as it sounds, no woman loves her post-natal body. Secondly, the weakness and aches of a post-natal body are overwhelming. Unless you overcome this mental barrier and get moving you might stay like this for many years to come. And a weak body means a weak mind. A weak woman means a weak mum.

It is my deep belief that every mum loses it at some point. That one day you get fed up and you want to be left alone, completely alone, just for a few hours. You need alone time to get your thoughts and feelings in the right order. That doesn't mean you don't love your family, quite the opposite, you love them too much and you ended up being drained by sacrificing yourself to the extreme. And now you are paying the price.

Looking good and having a strong body is needed by both your inner woman and you the mum. Don't think that just because you are a mum you will be comfortable being overweight or obese, no one is. I've been there and I know this. Don't think for a second that becoming complacent in a weak body is the answer to your happiness. I am not asking you to be a narcissist and overcompensate, but a minimum effort to keep you healthy and improve your stamina is required. When I started exercising again after having Junior I thought I was doing it for me. As I kept on exercising and coming back stronger I realised something else: I was actually doing it for him and my little family. The weight I gained during pregnancy caused me great pain. I worked so hard for years to have my dream body and in nine months I was back at my heaviest, 220 pounds. I was under so much emotional distress and to make things worse my biggest enemy, doubt, was back. I was doubting my capacity to lose all that weight again and not because I didn't know how to or my body was too weak, but I was scared I would get lost in the mum life and give up on myself like before.

For too long society has decided what a mum should or should not do. It is time to acknowledge your real value and claim the respect and appreciation you deserve. The reason why women lose touch with their inner self once they become mums is society. You are told that it is OK to be obese and depressed, you are a mum. It is OK to wear baggy clothes and look unattractive. It is OK to never put make-up on or do your hair and nails. It is OK to have sex once per year on your anniversary. After all, you are a mum and you don't have time to take care of yourself.

According to society the desire to satisfy your needs must cease to exist once a baby comes out of you. Switching off your inner woman is not the answer to happiness and freedom, but the most self-destructive action you can take against yourself. When you say you don't have time or that you don't care, that is not you speaking. It is the result of all the influences in your environment. When a mum says I can't or I don't have time she is lying. Mums are the most extraordinary creatures with an endless capacity to do and achieve.

I felt selfish when I started exercising again. I felt I was burdening my partner to watch the baby whilst I was exercising. I had doubts I could even pull through and stick to a routine. I had lots of fears and doubts. I took it one day at a time and coped with whatever came my way. And when I say cope I don't mean give up and lock myself in the house but to stand my ground for what matters to me, and I didn't allow opinions to influence my transformation journey. I started exercising again to lose the baby weight. I started exercising again to defeat my depression. I started exercising again to stay sane. And as I carried on I discovered many other advantages of exercising. It was the best way to release my anger and frustration. This made me more composed. It helped me discipline myself again in all areas of my life, not just fitness. For one hour whilst I was exercising I was a woman. Yet again, fitness saved me. This time fitness made me a better mum and saved my family.

From my experience there are two ways to look at exercising: beauty contest or life saviour. Your choice. Losing the baby weight was indeed important, but more importantly it was defeating the depression. The emotional pain, the mental burden and all those negative thoughts became unbearable. I had to get better or I was at risk of losing my family.

What are the benefits of exercising post-partum? Your body becomes stronger and your energy level will explode. Your brain produces endorphins so you are happy for a while. It allows you to eat real fucking food in decent sized portions. You regain your confidence. It improves your resistance and stamina, and you can actually play and keep up with your kid now. It improves your sleep and digestion. As a woman you feel light again, attractive, strong, capable of achieving. It increases the tolerance to stress. It is pure therapy for shitty days. You fit in your pre-pregnancy clothes. You own your womanhood and proudly stand naked in front of your partner. You can be a mum and a woman. You actually have time to care for yourself. That's just a few of the benefits I encountered following post-natal exercising. You can discover many others.

If I were to sum up all these benefits, I believe the most important one is this: exercising keeps you sane. I know you might have the strength to portrait the perfect life for the outside world, but you know how hard motherhood is. You know how often you feel overwhelmed and drained and just need a break from your reality. It is OK to admit it. If you never trained before and have no idea how brilliant the post-workout feeling is don't let that prevent you from starting post-partum. You are a mum, you are not dead, although your inner woman might have died a while ago due to pure neglect. Check out my entry level package for mums who are ready to shake the boat at www.superheromum.co.uk.

I want you to really understand this. Once you get that baby out you will forever be a mum. If you keep postponing your needs in the hope that one day your chores will end, well, keep waiting. You will never be just a woman again. Regardless what age the kids are, if you are used to living in sacrifice and give everything to your environment then you will never stop.

The needs and chores change but the subject performing them will still be you. So get that thought out of your head. How many years have you been waiting already? Stop delaying your comeback and start prioritising – today!

'I don't have time'. That's just mums' favourite excuse because there is always something keeping you busy. I mean hello? Is it not obvious I am running around all day? Perfectly credible excuse. If you want to truly change there are three steps you need to take:

- Make yourself a priority again
- Plan ahead
- Stay committed

Whatever excuse you have been using for years it is enough. Whatever thoughts you have been relying on to deceive yourself that you can be happy whilst living in sacrifice, forget them. Because you are reading this book I know you are done with bullshit. You are a grown ass woman seeking a solution to a long-lasting problem. Lucky you, the solution is finally here.

Unless you make time for yourself nobody will do so. Learn how to be selfish again. Here is a quick story. When I started taking my boy to nursery he didn't like it. In fact he hated it. He suffered from separation anxiety for a while and that made my anxiety shoot through the roof as well. For a good month I would sit in a coffee shop two minutes away from nursery and wait for him there. Most of this time I would cry, convincing myself that I am a horrible mum incapable of giving everything to my boy. That one month I wanted to pull him out of nursery every day, and if it wasn't for my partner I would have done so.

As the days passed he got used to the place and eventually started enjoying it. However, as part of his protest he would have his nap later than normal in the hope that I wouldn't take him to nursery. Even if he was waking up one hour before nursery closing time I would take him there. Again, I didn't want to do any of this and it was hurting me to know my boy was missing his mummy in there, but my partner, who is much saner than me, knew how much I needed a few hours away from Junior. Slowly, I started driving back home after dropping him off.

The reason why I am sharing this story with you is this: putting him in nursery was the best choice. Although it was emotionally draining and I felt guilty every minute along the way, I am fully enjoying my time off. I get to do work, train and live a balanced life. I have learned that being selfish made me a better mum. I miss my boy so much when he is in nursery, and when I pick him up he fills me with joy and love. And because I have achieved my own goals throughout the day and I am not drained I can offer him joy and love in return. As a mum I learned the hard way that the quality of the time you spend with your family matters, not the length. Long, stupid hours where you are depressed, obese, unhappy and hate your life, will not make you a better mum, ever.

So next time you use motherhood as an excuse for your inner pain think twice, if you want your kids to carry a burden which is not theirs to carry.

Chapter 13

Let's start a DIET

After years of trying, failing, giving up, wasting time and money, I came up with this definition to the word diet.

DIET = Die Trying

You must have tried low calorie diets, no carbs diets (which is a lie, there are carbs in almost anything you eat), skipping meals, skipping snacking, shakes, weight loss tea, magic pills, dehydration, laxatives, maybe forced vomiting… the list is long.

By exercising wise you must have done endless hours on the treadmill and whatever other cardio machines your significant other bought you as a present. Most likely you have invested many hours and money in Zumba and dancing classes.

And all you got from it was a big waste of time and money. Many attempts have been made and the results, if obtained, never lasted. Uh, you are a mum now. That means three things:

1. You must stay healthy
2. You are the role model
3. You don't have spare time

Your duty as a mum is to live healthily, take care of yourself and lead by example. As a child who grew up in a fucked up family, let me tell you something. I couldn't care less what my parents were telling me about weight loss and wasting my life overeating. And you know why? Because they were doing the exact opposite of their advice. Their lack of commitment to their own advice made any word coming out their mouths a big fucking lie. How can obese people with the worst eating habits try and educate me on making smarter choices? Complete fucking disaster.

Every day I see mums feeding their kids broccoli and taking them to all kinds of sports. They are young, they can't make their own choices yet, but once they grow up and get the right to choose what do you think their choice will be? If you forced the healthy lifestyle on them whilst you stuffed your face sitting on the sofa all evening, my guess is that those kids will end up overeating as young adults.

It is unfair to ask your kids to be someone you have failed to be. I get angry when I see obese mums being super proud of their kid's athletic accomplishments. I don't even want to imagine what that child feels like. Let's say the child plays tennis and he is really good and wins competitions and all. Don't you think he would love to play with his mum too? Not every day but now and then so he can show you how fantastic he is doing and maybe teach you some new moves. But you are so sad and overweight that all you can do is drive him to the tennis club and sit down watching him. Where is the role model part? Where is the active involvement in his development?

Not having time is not a good excuse to use anymore. With access to programmes online you can squeeze in a workout at any point throughout the day. You don't need to travel to any gym or find the right PT or waste time in traffic. All you need is literally one click away.

Also, recent studies have proved the efficiency of short, intense workouts compared to hours spent on the treadmill. Science has proved that thirty minutes of movement per day increases your life expectancy. Wake up early and do a quick session. Go to bed late but still do it. Just do it! There is nothing easier for a mum than filling your schedule with BS, useless chores. Everything you have to do can wait for twenty to thirty minutes. The reason why you are not moving your arse off the sofa is quite simple: you don't want it bad enough. You have given up on yourself and your ability to lead by example. You have become your worst nightmare.

You have to take control of your life. Stop being scared of failure and living your life in the darkness of the past. Yes, shit happened. Some choices were good, others not so much. Yes, you gave up. Every single attempt ended up in you being more frustrated. Blah, blah, blah. I have been there and I know each and every excuse you are going to use.

Summary

The times when mums were seen just as housewives have ended. The new era allows mums to be empowered and make their own choices. Be sexy and fit, strong and driven.

Fitness makes you a better mum. The physical and emotional benefits of training are endless. Learn how to be selfish again and make yourself a priority. Finding a positive hobby to express your anger and frustration will help tremendously with your sanity. And it will make you calmer.

I know every thought you are creating right now for the purpose of deceiving yourself. Shit happens, nobody's life is perfect. You are the only one who can take charge and write the rules by which you wish to live your new life. The reason why stuff didn't work in the past is simple. You were doing the wrong thing. Hours of cardio and starvation will not burn fat.

All it does is make you miserable, tired, hungry, angry and frustrated for putting the work in without actually getting any results. Listen. It's not your fault. You were sold on hearsay and women who like to punish themselves. Just because your friend is a fan of wasting time and never enjoys fucking real food, it doesn't mean you have got to do the same. If she jumps off a bridge would you? Thought so.

So let's recap. Stop living in fear of failure and buckle up for your greatest journey yet to start. What you need is a programme designed by a mum for mums. Every single struggle you are facing, I had my fair share of it too. And let me tell you this: you can do it. Remember, it's not about a diet, or die trying, it's about the lifestyle you create for yourself, and one you truly enjoy.

Chapter 14

Breastfeeding and weight loss

Before I start digging into this I want to clarify that all the information is based on my experience. Everything I share with you or any advice I give you is what I have learnt the hard way. You don't have to suffer like I did, just use the tips below to make weight loss and breastfeeding a breeze.

The general rule goes something like this: weight loss is impossible whilst breastfeeding. The biggest BS out there. I bet this myth was created by mums who were too lazy to put the work in and rather lie to themselves than take action. I have personally lost five stone whilst breastfeeding. And guess what? The opposite happened, breastfeeding actually helped me lose weight. When you feed your baby you burn calories. Yes, you have the apparatus to make milk, but the whole process is very demanding on your body and thus you burn extra calories.

Now there are two reasons why new mums believe that weight loss and breastfeeding don't go together: the quantity and quality of the milk might be affected. Yes and no. Indeed, you have to be smart about your nutrition and choice of training. Be smart about it but don't give up completely because you know, you have the perfect excuse. As I mentioned before the low calories or low carbs diets will not work for your anymore. If you breastfeed expressly you consume in between 300 to 500 calories more per day. So whatever your choice of eating, you must get those extra calories in. As such don't panic if you eat four meals per day and snack in between too. You need to make sure you get enough calories in for you and the baby, so don't stay hungry for too long throughout the day. Also, make sure you have a healthy snack on hand all the time. I know how hungry you can get whilst breastfeeding. Uh, and if you feed your baby through the night the hunger will be your alarm clock. Get your carbs in with the first meal of the day. It will give your body the fuel it missed through the night and put the feeling of hunger to rest.

Secondly, you want to provide your body with all the main nutrients, carbs, fat and protein. Why is that necessary? Because that is how you preserve the quality of the milk. Now there seems to be a lot of confusion regarding nutrition during breastfeeding. The most common one is that the mum has to eat everything and literally stuff her face to produce amazing milk. Let's stay here for one second. Everything you eat and drink goes into your milk, so from water to food the taste of the milk will reflect your eating habits. Therefore it is extremely difficult for me to understand why eating fast food is OK and provides good milk and having a steak with salad is affecting the quality of the milk. It's the other way around actually. Eating healthily will provide the best milk for the baby. Seriously, why would you want fast food to be the source of your baby's food? A healthy, balanced diet will not only make you look and feel amazing, but provide the best milk for your baby. I believe it's a win-win.

And I just shared with you the first two secrets to weight loss when breastfeeding. The third one is training. Your choice of training will have the final impact on your transformation journey. Choose the wrong one and not only will the weight loss will be extremely slow, but your breasts will hurt tremendously when training and, trust me, that puts anybody off. Before becoming a mum you probably used to do all kinds of dancing classes and spend hours on the treadmill. If your breasts are massive and full to the point that they leak everywhere, the kind of training just mentioned will cause great pain and discomfort to your chest area. So you have got to be smart about it.

These are the three tips that I personally used to reduce my breast discomfort whilst training: excess, wear the right sports bra and avoid jumping. In the first four months post-partum 1 was producing ridiculous amounts of milk. As such my breasts were hard and full most of the time. So I discovered that if I excess right before training they will feel lighter and ease my discomfort, thus allowing me to focus on my session. You are going to think that I am exaggerating but I would excess in the car in front of the gym right before going in. It made a huge difference to my comfort.

Secondly, make sure that you wear the right sports bra. After you give birth, if you choose to breastfeed your breasts will suddenly double or triple in size. I was like damn, I wanted these big boys for a quite a while and now I've got them for free. The problem with that is that your bra size will keep changing. And seriously, you have enough new expenses with the baby's arrival. Plus, you are losing weight and your clothing sizing changes every few weeks. I completely agree, but please learn from my mistake. As my partner says, 'stop being stingy when it comes to stuff that can actually ease your life'. For a while I didn't want to invest in new sports bras based on the reasons mentioned above. And I paid the price for it. The wrong size sports bra will allow those bad boys to move around and cause you horrible pain. Also, make sure it is a good quality one. The cheap ones stretch too much and don't do the job. It doesn't have to be the most expensive one, but a decent brand. Ah, and go and try it on in the shop. Your size will vary so much that eventually you will have no idea what your size actually is. And unless you want to keep ordering online and returning it until you get it right, a trip to the shop it is.

My third piece of advice is don't jump – too much or too high. The treadmill is a no-no. A skipping rope is a no-no. Dancing is a no-no. Any exercise which causes you discomfort substitute it with something else. A time will come when your body will be stronger and your milk supply regulated properly so you don't have to experience pain throughout your sessions. Until then accommodate your needs and make the whole experience as comfortable as possible. You are supposed to enjoy the change and its benefits, not make it the worst experience of your weight loss journey.

Summary

Breastfeeding and weight loss are possible. Learn the foundation of a healthy and balanced diet and your milk supply or quality of the milk will not be affected. Remember that all you eat and drink goes into your milk, and I highly doubt that you want your baby to get his nutrients from unhealthy sources.

Don't be scared to stop listening to the mums who failed to do better. Breastfeeding doesn't mean you have to stay overweight or gain even more weight. It doesn't mean you can't train. All you have to do is make smarter choices and surround yourself with people who will encourage and support you in your journey.

By using the tips above I guarantee that you will take charge of your weight loss journey and most of your discomfort and worries because they will disappear.

Chapter 15

Reason and excuse

This chapter is not for the light-hearted. It contains the brutally honest words of a mum who has been through hell and came back stronger than ever to change her life. I felt I had to dedicate a whole chapter to this reason and excuse topic. In the mum community excuses are the main reason why mums don't start their transformation journey and neglect the inner woman.

I want to start by providing my own definition of what an excuse is. An excuse is a lack of action to better yourself, a way of life for people who are unable to take charge of their lives and Assume responsibilitysponsibility for their shit.

A reason is what makes everything possible. Reason equals drive and the end result will always be achievement of the bigger goal. Reason beats excuse on any level because every excuse should be converted into a reason to push forward.

Mums are so fierce to state that their life is genuinely busy and hectic that every excuse they bring up is protected by the 'you don't understand my life' line.

I am doing this and this and this and it never ends. I never said you are not doing all those things. What I am saying is that you could do it differently.

You must learn how to take care of yourself again. The reason why you are feeling drained, overwhelmed and underappreciated is you. The moment you killed your inner woman and became just a mum things started going south. Even the most dedicated mums who dreamt of raising a herd of kids lose it at some point. You have got your own needs and unless you satisfy yourself first you will eventually resent your whole environment. It is easier to use everything as an excuse than dust off the victim attitude and take charge of your life.

Mums love routines. Why? Because subconsciously you calculate how much energy you need to invest in every activity. If anything takes you off your routine you panic. You will use that unforeseen event as an excuse for a very long time. Let's say you were trying to stick to an exercise plan and then your kid got a cold. And you had to care for the child who was home for a few days. And that put you off and took you off the priority list.

And now, two months later, you are not exercising anymore and the poor child's cold is still to blame. You see what I mean? Just because shit happens and you have to adapt to a new routine for a while doesn't mean you give up on everything you have achieved so far. Don't have the victim attitude and assume that you are the only one who has to cope with life. All mums have kids who get sick. The percentage of single mums increases by the day. Working mums are the norm. Some even have two jobs. People break up, lose jobs, face financial difficulties, suffer depression, get sick, die. That is life. Now you can choose whether you want to thrive or be a victim and never control your life.

Not only is a mum's life hectic on a normal basis, any additional change of circumstance is seen as the end of the world. Your inability to develop strong, positive coping mechanisms is what keeps bringing you down each and every time. Life is full of unforeseen events. Break-ups, sickness, deaths, getting fired, abuses, financial difficulties, depression, anxiety, disappointment, the list is endless. Life will always throw stuff at you. It is your choice if you want to stay strong and make the best decisions in the given circumstances, or sit down and feel sorry for yourself. Keep eating in the hope that emotional numbness will be achieved. That somehow food will make the pain disappear. If you are waiting for the right time get this clear: there is never a better time to start than now. Most of the time an event will trigger your change.

My health was poor when I started my transformation journey. All my tests showed the results of an aged body and I was only twenty-two years old. Everything was red on that paper. Instead of crying for my condition and feeling sorry that I ruined my health I chose to make smarter choices. From that point onwards I made the call to eat healthily and start training. It was the biggest decision I had made in years and trust me, it was about freaking time to regain control over my life. I needed an impetus and my lifestyle choices affecting my health was the last drop. There is always a positive to look out for even in the worst cases.

My grandma has had diabetes for thirty years now. My aunty got it a few years ago. My father got it recently. There is this general panic in the family that we are all going to get diabetes at some point down the line. There is a genetic predisposition to diabetes in my family. I accept that. My way of making sure I don't die of diabetes is to live a healthy life. I train, I move, I eat healthy, I treat my body as it deserves. I analysed my grandma's, aunty's and father's lifestyle. All of them are super lazy. They have never, ever exercised in any shape or form. Their eating habits are the worst. They have been morbidly obese for more than half their lives. That's at least thirty years of extra fat on the organs, extra effort on the joints to support the weight, and an overall extra effort for the body to function. No wonder they are exhausted all the time.

Observe how I made my family's genetics a reason to live a better life. The perfect excuse would have been this: diabetes runs in my family and no matter what I can't escape it. Or let me stuff my face with sweets because after I get diabetes I can't eat any. You might be laughing now but it is unfortunate how many think this way.

You made food your ally a long time ago. Let me share with you a number of questions to ask yourself to check if you still are in control of your habits or not.

1. Do you think of food all the time?
2. Do you always finish the food to the last bite?
3. Do you binge eat when stressed or upset?
4. Do you return to overeating every time shit gets hard?
5. Do you eat out of boredom?
6. Would you rather eat than engage in other activities?
7. Is food changing your emotions – positively or negatively?
8. Do you cry when you are on a strict diet?

9. Is food your main concern if you attend a party?
10. Would you spend your last penny on your favourite foods?

If more than half of the answers are YES you have a food addiction to fight. Addiction means you have lost control over that habit and you are not using your reasoning anymore before engaging in that activity. Therefore, it is out of your control. Secondly, your mind will fabricate excuses to ensure you don't regain control. Self-sabotage if you prefer. Just because you give it a fancy name doesn't make it OK. Think before putting your hand on food. Take a deep breath and engage your reasoning. Ask yourself this:

1. Am I truly hungry?
2. Will food remove my pain?
3. Will food make my life happy again?
4. Am I eating because of boredom?
5. How is food improving my situation?
6. Could I replace food with another activity to feel better?

I used to be addicted to food. I hated every piece entering my mouth and yet I felt as if I couldn't stop eating. Seeing my naked body in the mirror was causing me great pain. I was hating my body and myself for being weak. And I would overeat in the hope that the pain would disappear. Observe the never ending vicious cycle. I hated being obese but I kept on stuffing my face. I was hoping that stuffing my face would take the pain away. More eating meant I would gain even more weight. Which brings me back to the initial hate I had for my body. More weight gained meant more hate towards myself.

The most common excuses used by mums:
- I don't have time
- I am too tired
- I've got to watch the kids
- It is not for me
- I am a mum
- I have to clean
- I have to cook
- I have to do the laundry
- I have to do the dishes
- I have to do homework
- I have no energy left
- I don't have the discipline
- I don't have motivation
- I've lost my mojo
- I have errands to run
- My kids go first
- I can't afford a nanny

- I am depressed
- I suffer from anxiety
- I am scared
- I have tried already, it doesn't work
- I don't know where to start
- My partner is jealous
- My partner is not supportive
- My partner loves me just the way I am
- I am going through a separation
- The weather is cold
- The weather is hot
- My job is shit
- My manager is a dick
- I don't make enough money
- I have too much money
- I spend too much time in traffic
- I can't drive
- I can wear saggy clothes
- I've got stuff happening right now
- I will wait for the kids to grow older
- I need food for comfort
- I am single
- I am married
- I will wait for summer
- It is not the right time
- You don't understand my life
- I was raised in an obese family

- My body hurts when I train
- I don't have the right form
- What is the best exercise?
- What is the best diet?
- I have a sweet tooth
- I can't control myself around food

Are you bored yet? I know I am. The BS mums can come up with is amazing. Unbelievable!

You have used these excuses so many times that they have now become genuine reasons for you not to take action.

In reality there is only one reason why you don't go and book a call with me right now: fear of failure!

You are terrified that you will commit for a while and then regress again. You have tried so many diets and workouts in the past and despite getting results you haven't discovered a way to maintain those results. What if I told you that I can change your life forever? I believe in my system so much I guarantee you it is the answer to all your prayers.

I always say if there is a problem, fix it. If right now you are overweight, feeling heavy and sad about your body, underappreciated and overwhelmed by your environment, then make a change. Your current situation is sad already, how much worse can it get?

What is the real reason behind your lack of action? The thing with failure is this. I always tell my son that he can achieve whatever he wants. Saying things like 'I can't' must never be part of his vocabulary. The only reason why you haven't succeeded yet is because you haven't tried enough times. If nobody told you before that failure is good for your growth, I am doing it now.

Every failure brings a new lesson and every lesson brings you closer to success. Learn and grow, my dear. I had at least 100 attempts until I got it right. And every attempt came with disappointment and frustration, but also with valuable lessons. If I were to stop from trying to find my path I would never have succeeded.

All the excuses I have mentioned before are used on a daily basis by mums around the globe. When I hear you saying that you cannot achieve or commit it is not you talking. As a mum you have the ability to accomplish the most incredible things. When my son is doing some nonsense and I have to rush to catch him and save his life, I have this joke that I could defeat Usain Bolt in that moment. Mum power is highly underestimated. When it is something related to your kids you are not a regular human anymore. All your instincts are awakened and that gives you the strength to achieve amazing things. Who told you that you cannot be happy again? Who told you that you cannot look freaking fabulous again? Who told you that you don't have what it takes to live a balanced life where you are a mum and a woman?

I want you to use the same energy for yourself. You are a brilliant mum and you want to do better, that's why you are reading this book. Stop being scared! What is the real reason behind your excuse? Are you scared of failure, of change, that your transformation will take too long? Are you not ready to defeat your inner pain and take charge of your present? Or perhaps you don't know where to start and how to make things work. Go to my website www.superheromum.co.uk and start your transformation right now. My platform is not designed for professional athletes but for mums who want to feel and look amazing.

The most common excuse mums use is this: I don't have time. I know you believe that is true and it is not an excuse, but let's look at it in detail. You can't get more than twenty-four hours per day. What you must do is use your time more efficiently. If you want to have more time you have to learn to maximise and prioritise in your daily responsibilities. Take one minute and think your day through. How much time do you spend doing nothing because you are too tired to engage? How much time do you waste on insignificant chores? I bet you love to watch a two-hour movie every night. Or catch up on some entertainment shows, after all, you deserve to relax after a stressful day. Oh, and whilst you are at it snack on junk as well. That's two hours! Do you know how much time you need to do my training programme? One hour per week, which is less than 1% of your weekly time. One hour out of 168 hours you have in a week! The reality is that you don't want it bad enough.

Time is not an issue, your inability to prioritise and focus on what really matters prevents you from making smarter choices. You are in charge of everybody's schedule in the house and you must use your power. Being overwhelmed is easy. Being in control and owning your life requires skills. You must always run your day and never let the day run you. When I gave birth to our son Oli was working sixteen hours a day. I had no friends or family to help me so I was literally taking care of everything myself. I was managing the house with all the cooking and cleaning, I was running all errands, and of course looking after the baby. Also, I would delegate a few hours per day towards running the gym. Oh, and I was training and living healthily too. And for six months I was suffering from post-natal depression and anxiety. I often wonder how I managed all that. The answer is a burning desire to be better and by prioritising. When you have a definite goal you are unstoppable. And that's when you stop making up excuses and convert everything in your life in a reason to grow.

Let me tell you how I managed back then. I would do my grocery shopping online and get it delivered at 7 am, which meant I could schedule my day freely and didn't have to stay in the house to wait for the delivery. Because we were eating healthily cooking wouldn't take too long, so I would sort that out in the first part of the day. As a mum I am all about multi-tasking, so before cooking I would throw a load in the washing machine. Whilst cooking I would probably clean a little bit and boom, by noon the house is sorted. All this time I am holding the baby and getting him tired for his nap. By noon baby is ready to sleep, food is done, laundry is sorted, house is in a decent shape. Junior was only sleeping on my chest so I was pinned down during his nap. I would take this time to read, catch up with the business or make any phone calls required. As soon as Junior was up we would go run whatever errands we had and then go straight to the gym. There I would replace Oli for a few hours and if time allowed he would watch Junior whilst I was training, if not I would train and watch Junior myself and run the gym. Looking back now it was not easy, but discipline and planning helped a lot in those extremely busy times.

Despite the odds, the times when I achieved the most were all extremely busy times or extremely sad times when some tragic event happened. I converted everything in a reason to thrive. Defeating my depression, losing the baby weight, learning how to be a great mum and wife for me constitute the perfect reason to keep pushing. On the other side I was at my lowest when everything in my life was the perfect excuse not to take positive action. What happened in between? I developed healthy coping mechanisms. No more binge eating and feeling sorry for my life, no more wasting time on useless activities and no more victim attitude. I created a better environment. I surrounded myself with positive people who are taking action to improve every day. I took control of my life. Everything happens because of me, not to me, by random luck or bad lack. I understood that fear is normal. The only way to grow is to act outside my comfort zone. I acknowledged my true value. I am worthy of love and respect and I don't accept anything less. Life is hard. There will always be challenging times to face.

A better you is capable of achieving greater things. Learn how to manage motherhood. Learn how to take care of your inner woman. Make smart choices so you can live a happy life. Make smart choices so your kids can live a happy life. Use irrational reasons to make your life better. The same way you have created millions of excuses throughout your life, now it's time to create reasons.

Summary

Stop hiding behind excuses and face your fears. Use everything in your life as a reason to thrive, not an excuse to be complacent and live a life less than satisfactory. Mum life is hectic and there is always something to do and someone to attend. Unless you learn how to prioritise you will continue to feel drained.

Taking action now will soon give you that energy and strength you lost a long time ago. Don't let the fear of failure, fear of getting out of your comfort zone, fear of waking up your inner woman stop you from growing as a person and ultimately becoming the greatest mum you can be.

You are the role model. Unless you become strong and take charge of your environment your kids will not develop the necessary skills to thrive later in life. Develop healthy coping mechanisms so the next time life hits you hard you will move forward and not regress.

Become a reason and stop being an excuse!

Chapter 16

Big fat lies

The world has changed dramatically in the last decade. Access to information is faster and easier than it has ever been. Literally one click away. Data is usually unlimited and accessible on all devices. I dare to say information spreads across the globe faster than lightning striking Earth. With impressive speed and volume there are problems too. The information is not controlled anymore, and anybody can say or post anything online. That means two things: information is not accurate and reliable anymore and marketing has no limits.

Marketing in the twenty-first century has reached a whole new level. A company set up on one side of the world can easily sell to the opposite side of the planet. The power of online marketing is unlimited.

As expected, the fitness industry has grown massively. Why do I say as expected? Because every day people become more shallow. Any woman you pick out of the 3.5 billion on the planet would want to change something about her appearance. How did we get here? Free access to everything! Hell, I want new boobs too. After nearly two years of breastfeeding no chest exercise is going to repair the damage.

At the same time the reasonable me is like 'why would you endanger your life and voluntarily have surgery? Have you lost your mind?' There is a duality when it comes to the perfect body. And this duality is highly abused by the market. Your weakness became their best selling point.

The fitness industry is full of big fat lies. And that's because big companies cash in on your failure. Every time you try a new product, a new shake, a new supplement, a new workout, somebody makes money. And the more you try and fail, the more money you spend. And now comes the real question: if you find a solution to your problem you would stick to it, wouldn't you? And that means you stop looking for other things and thus stop spending money. This is the boogie man for the industry.

As such there is lots of BS to choose from. Too many diets to keep up with, too many shakes, too many exercising plans, too much of everything.

I know for a fact that you have tried quite a few of these things yourself. Any woman, regardless of her weight or appearance, has tried to detox, eat healthier, reduce the fat percentage, get a flat stomach for an event and so forth. However, you don't seem to be able to put yourself together and do it again now as a mum.

Or you have attempted but the stuff which worked before is impossible to stick to now. Which mum can live on 500 calories per day long-term? Or have only shakes to keep her going through the day? And perhaps you got to the conclusion that being a mum doesn't allow you to take care of yourself anymore. And that means two things: you have given up completely or you will wait a good few years for the kids to grow older. Both options are equally bad.

I gave up on myself before. I accepted my pain and said to myself I was born to be fat and unhappy. With every failed attempt I would end up being more frustrated and gaining more weight. So I started to eat like never before. I'm talking HUGE quantities of food every day.

I remember Saturday night six years ago. As usual I dragged my fat self out for a night of booze and dance with my girls. By the end of the night it was tradition to recharge the batteries at the nearby restaurant. You know, the kind of food which tastes so good at 4 am in the morning. We were seated at a table waiting for our order and next to us was a large group of people. I could see the waiter approaching with a large tray of food and I remember whispering to my friend, 'please tell me this is not ours… this is embarrassing.' Fortunately, the order was for the table next to us.

A few moments later I could hear the table next to us raising their complaints about the order. And that's when I realised that all that food was indeed ours. You will not believe this, we ordered ten meals of burgers and fries. That's right, that was the behaviour of a woman who gave up fighting for herself. From the moment I gave up on myself I continued on this path for a whole year. As a result I gained forty-four pounds. I was miserable.

My depression became permanent and I was completely lost. Every aspect of my life, university, work, relationships, everything was a mess. I had no direction. I was drowning in my own pain more and more every day. Giving up on yourself will bring more pain to your life than ever before.

Dear mum, giving up on yourself is the worst thing you can do. From that point onwards every aspect in your life will fall apart and you will be lost. You will seem to be alive but your inside will be rotten. Without goals, a desire to be better and a direction in life, you cease to exist. If you are at this point in your life when you think that giving up is the solution to your problems, think it through again. This is not a solution but major self-sabotage. By the time you realise the damage you created, it might be too late. As long as you breathe you must fight.

The second thing you do when everything has failed is to wait for the kids to grow older so you have more time to yourself. This mentality is so wrong. As the kids grow up they need a sane, fit mum able to cope with their needs and demands. If you spend a good five years of their lives being depressed and overweight and unable to engage in activities with them you're not the best role model.

Within these five years you might give up on yourself completely. Waiting is not always the best way to go about it. Instead of waiting and living a life where you feel overwhelmed, drained, depressed, unhappy and unfulfilled, why not find a solution to your problem and take charge of your life?

The two outcomes mentioned above must be avoided at all costs. That is the funeral of your inner woman. Being a mum is not all about sacrifice and giving, you must save some energy for yourself. Think of your past. Every time you tried to lose weight before perhaps it worked for you. And you proudly showed off those results. What happened after your diet finished? You gained all the weight back and more. That is the lesson you should have learnt from all your previous diets. It is not you being weak and lacking the discipline to carry on, diets are temporary. A diet cannot substitute a lifestyle. So instead of hanging on to your past and allowing it to be a disability in your present, why not seek a sustainable lifestyle which will allow you to feel and look amazing without resenting the process? Check out my Elite Superhero Mum Programme superheromum.co.uk/package. It is designed to help you build a lifestyle that fits in with your hectic life and allows you to take care of yourself in less than 1% of your weekly time.

Juicy diets are good if you want to clean your colon and detox your body. A detox is what it is. It is a temporary diet where you restrict your intake of solids and heavy foods so you clean your body of toxins. I've done that too. But I'm not a big fan. What do you do for the rest of the year though? You can't keep sipping on the juice. When I hear mums putting guilt on themselves for not being able to stick to juicy diets for longer, honestly, it makes me mad.

No human can live a happy, balanced life by drinking fruits and veggies. It doesn't provide enough fuel for the body and, make no mistake, your body will soon show you the consequences . And yet you fall for it and have high hopes just because a marketing campaign portraits it as a permanent weight loss solution.

You need to build a lifestyle. As a mum your life is exponentially more stressful than before. I personally don't know a single mum who doesn't suffer some kind of anxiety. You worry all the time, you want to do everything by yourself all the time, you are the one solving everybody's crisis. What I am trying to say is that you are more likely to binge eat as a mum than before.

And depriving your body of solid foods for a long period of time will make you so hungry that you will give in eventually. So you need a sustainable eating plan where you can actually control your hunger, impulses and stress tolerance level.

Supplements are the biggest scam out there. There is no shake which burns fat. It is a supplement to aid your meal plan and help you reach a calorific goal, there is no magic powder out there to burn fat for you whilst you watch TV and sit on the sofa. The reason why I refer to supplements is because of the strong marketing behind them. Whenever I'm in the gym I can easily count how many people drink plain water.

Most people in there, females and males, have shakes or colourful drinks. Let me explain something. There is no medical evidence that a shake enhances your fitness, endurance or increases your performance. It is a trend and it just looks cool to have colourful drinks.

If you don't do any kind of exercising and keep trying supplements in the hope that one day your extra weight will miraculously disappear, stop wasting your time and get to work. If you are a vegan or a vegetarian and you need protein shakes to ensure the right intake of protein, it serves a purpose there. But treat it as the supplement which it is and don't expect weight loss results solely because you are having shakes.

Many mums worry they can't lose weight without supplements. I have lost 150 pounds and never had any supplements. I learned how to eat and train in order to get results. Supplements are a choice, not a must, in your transformation journey.

I love intermittent fasting and it gives amazing results. It is simple and it works. Done over short periods of time it is not a danger to your health. Trying to extend that period of time and making it a lifestyle will eventually impact your health.

Intermittent fasting is good to understand your real hunger and kick start a quick fat burn. It works wonders, however, it is not a long-term solution for your weight loss journey.

The list of diets and options is too long to address here. Many of them work well in the short-term and give results. But what happens after the diet is finished? Most of the time you gain that weight back and even more. When your mindset is not right and you are only seeking to achieve quick results your WHY is not strong enough to keep you going through those days when you feel you can't commit anymore. Remember, everything in life is a choice. If you consciously make the decision to go for a quick fix then don't complain that one week later you are overeating again.

I have been you, I know exactly what you are going through every day. You can hide behind many excuses and deceive yourself in many ways, but the reality is that you need to get your shit right. You have to make better choices, if not for you then make them for your family.

Summary

Make an informed decision. Read how other people have succeeded in their quest to lose weight. Learn and apply. Don't take advice from people who have never tried anything or they did it the wrong way. I made my own mistakes which delayed my results. If I had advised people then I would have been completely wrong and would have possibly prevented somebody from becoming better.

Quick fix diet works short-term. If you have a massive amount of weight to lose you want to opt in for a sustainable meal plan to ensure results. If you wish to lose only a few pounds and the quick fix diet works wonders for you how do you maintain your weight afterwards? Plan and execute. Don't throw yourself head-first into a diet which eventually will make you more frustrated and depressed than when you started.

Find a way which you enjoy... love, I daresay. You cannot build a healthy lifestyle on a meal plan or by doing exercises which you despise. It is one thing to give it time to get used to the new routine, and a completely different one to hate what you do on a daily basis.

Losing weight is part of a transformation journey where you let go of your pain and negative emotions. You don't just get physical results, but you are becoming a happier, better person every day.

The reason why you haven't succeeded yet is because you haven't tried enough times!

THE SUPERHERO MUM MOVEMENT

After having my son and finding myself at my lowest, it took great effort and a burning desire to recover, to find my path again.

And as I looked around me I realised something major. Mums are the superheroes. All kids see their mums as the most beautiful and protective creatures, capable of endless love and sacrifice. But when it comes to their own needs mums pretend they are fine, they don't need anything.

That's how the SUPERHERO MUM MOVEMENT was built. It started with my conviction that mums deserve more. And by adhering to my path I will show you how to rejuvenate, lose weight, get a stronger body, be focused on your goal, change your mindset fully and regain your confidence and belief, and that you are capable to achieve great things.

I will initiate your journey from pain to power. Healthy eating, exercise, meditation, inner healing, aligning your body, mind and soul for one purpose: to wake up your inner woman and thus allow YOURSELF to exist and feel again!

If you made it all the way here you are ready to change.

Go to www.superheromum.co.uk and join the movement.

You can find me on social media:

Facebook: Stef Superhero mum
Instagram: stefsuperheromum
Email: stef@superheromum.co.uk

REACH YOUR FULL POTENTIAL

Imagine what your life could be if you had all the tools to transform and upgrade in every aspect.

SHM is an online coaching platform designed to guide you through the ultimate transformation. Starting with your mind, I will provide you with all the tools to upgrade your body and your life.

You will learn how to create and keep healthy positive habits, push your body to reach it's true potential and stay accountable to yourself and others.

Get started today! Visit

SUPERHEROMUM.CO.UK

Or call:
UK: +44(0)121 318 1734
US: +1 (786) 220 4703

S H M

Find your inner woman

All the tools you need to look and feel your best

superheromum.co.uk